An Unauthorized
Handbook and
Price Guide

Elsie® the Cow
and Borden's® Collectibles

Albert & Shelly Coito

Schiffer Publishing Ltd®

4880 Lower Valley Road, Atglen, PA 19310 USA

Dedication

We would like to dedicate this book to our fathers—

Albert J. Coito, Sr., who worked two jobs to support his family and still created incredible, lasting childhood memories. You have been nothing short of the perfect role model. I can only hope to be half the man you are.

And, Norbert S. Avila, who worked for Borden's for 33 years—leaving in 1940 to serve his country and returning to the Borden's Company in 1946—and is a Pearl Harbor Survivor. You taught your daughters pride in themselves and their work, but mostly added laughter to their days.

Copyright © 2000 by Albert & Shelly Coito
Photography by Dennie Farris Photrography
Library of Congress Catalog Card Number: 99-68179

Book Design by Anne Davidsen
Type set in Impress /Humanst521 BT

ISBN: 0-7643-1072-0
Printed in China
1 2 3 4

Published by Schiffer Publishing Ltd.
4880 Lower Valley Road
Atglen, PA 19310
Phone: (610) 593-1777; Fax: (610) 593-2002
E-mail: Schifferbk@aol.com
Please visit our web site catalog at
www.schifferbooks.com

This book may be purchased from the publisher.
Include $3.95 for shipping.
Please try your bookstore first.
We are interested in hearing from authors
with book ideas on related subjects.
You may write for a free catalog.

In Europe, Schiffer books are distributed by:
Bushwood Books
6 Marksbury Ave.
Kew Gardens
Surrey TW9 4JF England
Phone: 44 (0)208 392-8585; Fax: 44 (0)208 392-9876
E-mail: Bushwd@aol.com
Free postage in the UK. Europe: air mail at cost.
Try your bookstore first.

Contents

Special Thank You's
4

Introduction
5

A Brief History of Borden's and Elsie the Cow
6

Chapter One
Borden's, the Early Years
8

Chapter Two
Advertisement Signs, Items & Products
36

Chapter Three
Promotional Items & Related Collectibles
83

Chapter Four
Original Art Work & Unique Items
148

Special Thank You's

We would like to extend our sincerest appreciation and a big THANK YOU to the following people: Dennie Farris, for the fabulous photography and great conversation—your time and expertise was so much appreciated; Whitey Nottke, for the wonderful day we spent talking with you and your wife and looking at all the neat Borden's memorabilia; David Reid, for taking the time and patience to provide me with all the wonderful information and details regarding the original artwork; my parents, Albert and Margaret Coito, who, as I was growing up, not only introduced me to my passion of collecting but had to put up with all my "stuff" and "junk" on their dining room table, in their attic, garage, barn, on the porch, and anywhere else I could find till I got married and passed that frustration on to my wife. Thank you also, Mom and Dad, for all the love and encouragement you have given Shelly and me. To Mom and Dad Avila, thanks for opening your closets once in a while to give me quick peeks at all the cool stuff you think I'm always out to grab and for having a terrific daughter. To the rest of our family, thank you for all the support and encouragement you have given us. To Peter Schiffer and Jen Lindbeck, for your time, patience, and help in making this book a reality. Last but not least, thank you to our children, Sara Katelyn and Albert Joseph, your smiles make it all worth while.

Introduction

RRRing!!! The alarm clock sound shatters your rock, solid sleep as you roll over and hit the off button. It is 2:15 a.m. on a Sunday morning and you have exactly 30 minutes to get dressed and hit the road in hopes of being the first collector at a weekend antique street fair. Yes, while most people are sound asleep in the comfort of their warm beds, collectors are strategically planning their attack. Searching and building a collection takes time, and even though it is a hobby for most people, you can always find many collectors planning their free time and vacations around flea markets or antique shows. The main reason for all this craziness is simple: you are a collector and you are searching for that unique item or great buy to add to your collection. For us that is Borden's and Elsie the Cow.

For over twenty years now I have been collecting everything from milk bottles, old toys, old advertisements, and, my favorite, Borden's and Elsie the Cow. When I was a little boy, my father used to drive a milk truck. My older brother and I would ride along with him and love every minute of it. All the dairies that delivered to Borden's would have a large, die-cut, bright-eyed, smiling Elsie the Cow surrounded by a big yellow daisy. Oh the memories! I always loved that smiling cow. When I was sixteen years old I decided to keep my collections down to a few really special items and one of those was Borden's. When I met my wife and learned that her father worked for Borden's for 33 years, I knew we were meant for each other.

In the 1940s and 1950s, Borden's, like many other companies during that time, went wild in their advertisement departments. Borden's put out many promotional items with Elsie the Cow and her family. Stores were lit up with neon signs and fountains had banners, menu boards, menus, and easel-back advertisements. Even billboards on the highways contained Elsie and her family selling one of America's favorite desserts, ice cream. This book attempts to cover a wide range of those promotional items, company advertisement pieces, and "go-withs." There is so much out there yet to be discovered. We hope that this book helps to surface those never-before-seen items.

Our collection has truly brought us much happiness, many friends, and some wonderful memories that we hope to pass along to our children. As you flip through the pages of our collection, we hope that part of this book will take you on a sentimental journey back to your childhood. Enjoy!

A Brief History of Borden's and Elsie the Cow

The Borden Company© was named after its founder, Gail Borden who was born in New York in 1801. Mr. Borden supported himself with several different careers and in his spare time tinkered with new inventions. Eventually, through trial and error he discovered his most famous invention, a product he called "Condensed Milk," patented on August 19, 1856. On May 11, 1857, in an abandoned mill in Burrville, Connecticut, he opened for business as 'The Gail Borden, Jr., and Company©.' The company grew slowly until the beginning of the civil war in 1861. Government orders piled in for Borden's condensed milk to help feed the Union Army troops. To better distinguish between his high-quality product and other inferior brands, Borden created his American bald eagle trademark and named his product "Eagle® brand." After Gail Borden's death, in 1874, control passed to his sons. The company began selling milk in 1875 and also was the first company to sell milk in bottles in 1885. As the nineteenth century came to a close, the company was known as 'The Borden Condensed Milk Company©.' In 1919, Borden's changed its name to 'The Borden Company,' as they became more involved with other non-dairy related merchandise.

Although Borden's had previously advertised with cartoon cows, it wasn't until the 1939 New York World's Fair that Elsie became the official, famous spokescow for Borden's. In 1940, when the fair reopened, Elsie had her own boudoir decorated with a four poster bed and milk related accents. When Elsie had to leave the Borden exhibit to co-star in the film, *Little Men*, her husband, Elmer, was created to take her place at the exhibit. Elsie returned to the exhibit with a new addition to the family, Beulah.

With Elsie's popularity at an all-time high, and to meet the demands of her fan's, a traveling bedroom was created for Elsie and her family to tour the country. She visited numerous states helping to raise money for various charities. Elsie also helped win WWII by selling War Bonds and Stamps for the United States. In Europe, Elsie had a U.S. bomber named after her called *The Milk Run*, with Elsie's picture painted on the side. Elsie's family grew in 1947 with the birth of her son Beauregard. Again, in 1957, in celebration of Borden's One Hundredth Year, Elsie gave birth this time to twin calves, Larabee and Lobelia. Elsie and her family were very popular indeed and were one of the main attractions at Freedomland—an amusement park in New York built in the shape of the United States—from 1960 to 1963. It is easy to say that Elsie is one of America's most famous cows.

1904, Borden Condensed Milk Co. book mark, 6" x 2". $50-60. Borden Condensed Milk Co. changed its name to The Borden Company in 1919.

1939, Borden's Chateau Cheese booklet, 6.25" x 3", with early Elsie design. $15-20.

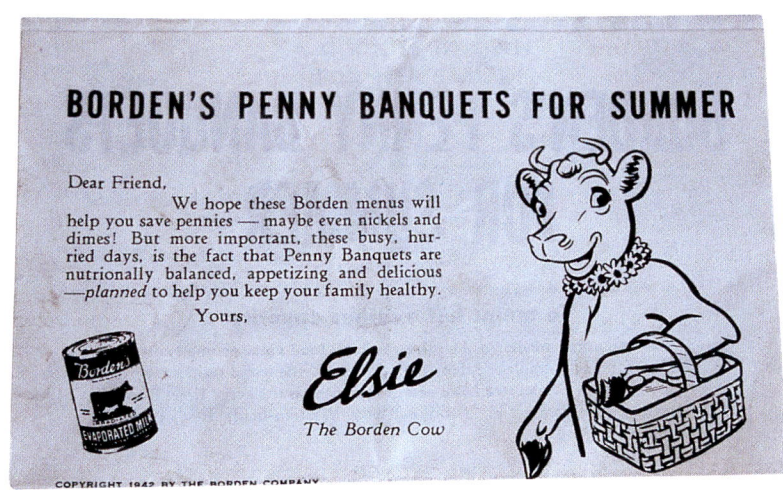

1942, Elsie Penny Banquet booklet, 5" x 3". $15-20. The changes you see here in Elsie's features were adopted in late 1941.

1949 recipe booklet, 5" x 3". $15-20. After WWII Elsie changed again. She kept this look into the 1960s, which overlapped with the next design of Elsie that came out in 1951.

Throughout her popularity Borden's marketing department changed Elsie's look several times. Her facial features and body began to resemble a more cow-like appearance and later she was changed into a more feminine, delicate, and animated Elsie. In 1951, the famous yellow daisy design was added behind Elsie's head. In the late 1960s, Borden's decreased its use of Elsie as an animated spokescow, but continued to use her as a well-known trademark. In 1968, Borden's added a rectangular, rounded cornered design to the 1951 daisy logo and connected the R and D in 'Borden,' which stand for Research and Development. As an American advertisement icon Elsie is still recognized and appears on a variety of consumer products.

1968 Borden's logo. Notice how the 'R' and 'D,' which stand for research and development, are connected.

1956 Brooklyn Dodger schedule, 6.5" x 4", with the famous, 1951 daisy logo around Elsie's head. $30-35.

Chapter One
Borden's, the Early Years
Early 1900s-1939

Borden's advertising memorabilia dating from the 1860s began with the trademark of an American bald eagle used on 'Eagle Brand' condensed milk. This symbol reflected the high quality and integrity of Gail Borden, Jr. and the Borden Company.

Those standards continued as Elsie's popularity grew in 1939 at the New York World's Fair, where she made her first appearance. Of course, Borden's products were always very popular and now it didn't hurt that they also had the public's attention with the most popular cow in America as their advertising icon. From the American eagle to the beginnings of Elsie the Cow, Borden's marketing department took off!

1900s paper advertisement fan for Borden's Condensed Milk Co., 13" tall. $125-150.

1900s cardboard, stand-up display for Borden's malted milk, 5" tall. $45-65.

Late 1900s glass Baby Brand Condensed Milk jar in original box, 4.5" tall. $75-95.

Two advertisement pocket mirrors from the late 1900s, 2" in diameter. $75-95 each.

1900s Borden's Evaporated Milk cardboard shipping box, 9" tall x 18" long. $45-50.

Three vintage Evaporated Milk cans with paper labels. One-pound can on the left, c.1900s, 4.75" tall, $45. Middle can, six ounces, 1920s, 2.5" tall, $25-30. 1920s, one-pound can on the right, 4.5" tall, $45.00

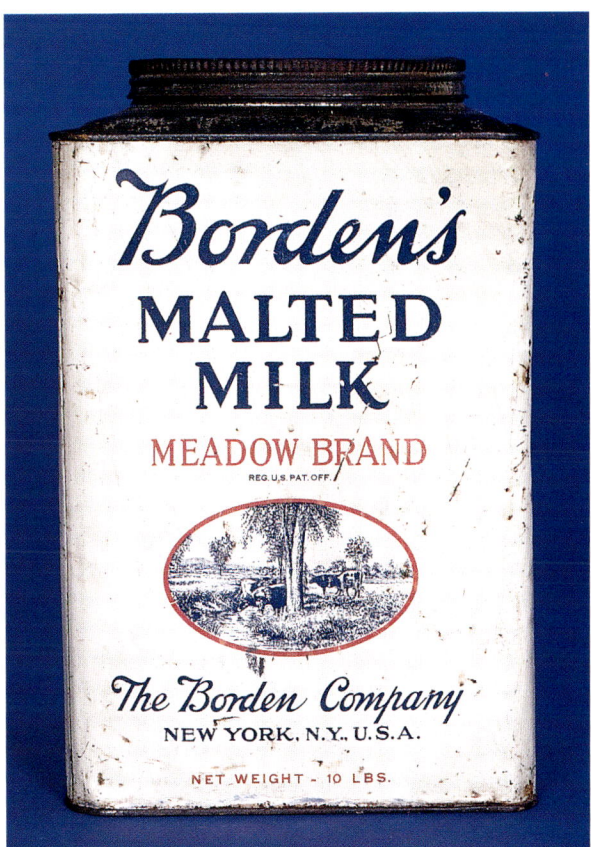

1920s, ten-pound, metal Borden's Malted Milk can, 11" tall x 7" wide. $50-60.

Metal 1920s, twenty-five pound, Borden's Malted Milk can, 15" tall x 8" wide. $50-60.

1920s, twenty-five pound Borden's Malted Milk can, 14" tall x 9.5" wide. $50-60.

1930s Borden's Eagle Brand, five-pound malted milk can, 10" tall x 5.5" wide. $35-40.

1930s Borden's Beta Lactose, 'An Improved Milk Sugar,' one-pound can, 3.5" tall x 4" diameter. $30-40.

Two Borden's whipping glass jars from the 1930s. Fourteen-ounce jar on the left, $65-85. Thirty-ounce jar on the right, $100-125.

Two 1930s glass malted milk containers with original lids.
Jar on left, 6.5" tall; jar on the right, 5" tall. $45 each.

Late 1900s-1930s postcard of the Borden's
milk plant located in Modesto, CA. $10-15.

Borden's Condensed Milk Factory, Modesto, Cal.
4368

1930s-1940s Borden's Golden Crest milk wagon toy, by Rich Toys. Metal and wood, 20" long x 9.5" tall. $350-400. Miniature case of Borden's milk bottles originally came with these wagons, 2" tall. $75-100. (*Note:* Golden Crest was a special brand of milk produced by Borden's.)

1920s milk wagon toy, by Rich Toys. Metal and wood, 17" long x 8.5" tall. $300-350.

Golden Crest milk wagon, 1930s-1940s, by Rich Toys. Metal and wood, 18" long x 8" tall. $300-350.

This wagon was made during WWII by Rich Toys out of paper and wood because of the metal shortage at that time. Side reads 'Buy War Bonds and Stamps.' $200-250.

Cute Borden's milk barn toy made out of wood, all original with silo. Manufactured in the 1930s-1940s, company unknown. Barn: 11.5" tall x 10.5" long; silo: 10" tall. Barn with silo: $150-200. Paper stand-up milk wagon in front of barn, 1930s, 5" long x 2.5" tall. $20-25.

In the late 1930s Borden's came out with this bright red and blue, checkerboard pattern for their product containers. One-pound cottage cheese container, $20-25. Five-pound cottage cheese container, $45-50. Egg carton, $35-40. Melorol ice cream box, $30-35. Ice cream nut roll, $30-35. All containers pictured are cardboard.

Rare and hard to find, modern quart, cream-top bottles with checkerboard design, all from California, dated 1940. $150-175 each. Half-gallon round bottle in center is also a California bottle dated 1940. $325-350.

1930s Malted Milk green glass jar, with original box, 6.5" tall. $65-75.

1930s Miniature 'Silver Cow' milk can, a salesman sample, 2.5" tall. $30-40.

From left: 1930s Creamed Cottage Cheese cardboard five-pound container, 5" tall. $35-40. Sweetened Chocolate Flavored Malted Milk tin, with paper label, 7.5" tall. $45-50. Small, one-pound, Malted Milk tin, 5.5" tall. $35-40.

1920s-1930s hand-painted wood sign, 'Borden's Ice Cream,' 30" long x 18" tall. $250-300.

1920s-1930s hand-painted oval wood sign, 'Borden's Ice Cream,'
29.5" long x 17.5" tall. $250-300.

1930s, 'Enjoy Borden's Ice Cream...it's real food,' reverse painted, glass display sign, made to either hang on the wall or as a stand-up, 21" long x 12" tall. $300-350.

Adorable! 1930s cardboard, stand-up ice cream display, 27" tall x 22" wide. $175-200.

1930s 'Borden's Malted Milk' dispenser. Top section is glass and base is green porcelain. $750-1,000.

Five different stainless malted milk containers used in soda fountains for powdered malt flavoring, 8" tall. $150-175 each.

1930s small round malted milk jar, embossed 'Borden's,' 6" tall. $125-150. Large round candy jar, embossed 'Borden's,' 11" tall. $225-250.

Large, round candy container with porcelain plate used in soda fountains to hold Borden's Tip Top Caramels, 11" tall. $350.

1930s Borden's butter crock, used in fountains or restaurants, 5.5" tall. $175-200.

Diner cup and saucer with Borden's logo, made by Shenango China, PA. $75-90.

Store cheese display, late 1930s, 21" tall. $175-200.

Cardboard, two-pound cheese box from the 1930s. $25-30.

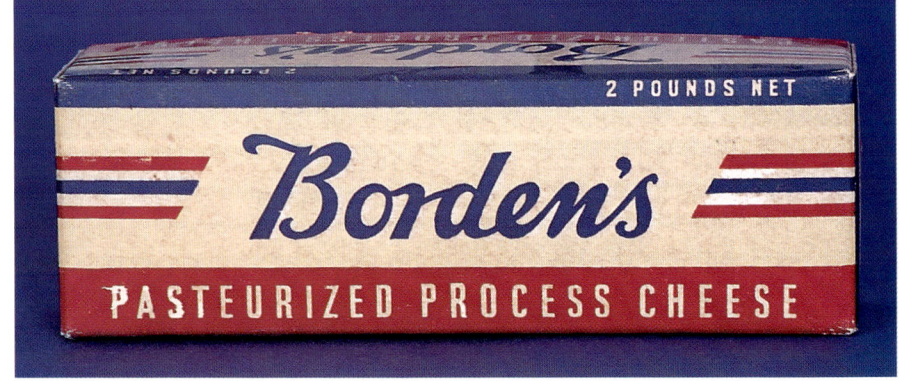

1940s long neck, wide-mouth 'Borden's Associated Companies' *(available nationally)* one-gallon milk bottles, 12" tall. These bottles are very hard to find. $350-450.

1940s standard style, wide-mouth gallon 'Borden's Associated Companies' *(available nationally)* milk bottles, 10" tall. $350-400.

Half-gallon, round milk bottles, both 9" tall, 1940s. One on the right is from Phoenix, AZ, hence the cacti. $75-100.

Borden's 'Golden Crest' quart milk bottles from Capitol Dairy Co., Sacramento, CA. Modern, cream-top bottle on left, $75-85. Standard quart on the right, $45-50.

1940s standard style, wide-mouth gallon Borden's milk bottle from Capitol Dairy Co., Sacramento, CA. $400-450.

Five different sizes and styles of Borden's milk bottles with delivery boy logo on front. Capitol Dairy modern cream-top bottle, $75-85. Four Dairy Delivery Co. bottles from San Francisco, CA. Standard quart, $45-50. Pint bottle, $30-35. Half-pint and quarter-pint, $20-25 each.

1930s-1940s Deluxe metal separator spoon for the cream-top bottles. When inserted into the throat of the bottle, this separator spoon made it easier for you to get the rich cream for your cereals or coffee from the top, bubbled section of the bottle. Spoons where given to customers compliments of their milkman. $50-60 in original box.

1930s-1940s Cream separator spoons, cardboard version, used as a throw away cream separator for the cream-top bottles. Given to customers compliments of their Borden's milkman. $25-30 in original box.

26

Twelve 1930s-1940s cream-top milk bottles with dairy delivery boy logo on front. Pictured is the back side of the bottles to show their various promotions and advertisement slogans for their products. $50-60.

Standard quart bottles with dairy delivery boy logo on front. Back of the bottles also came with product promotions. $30-40.

Late 1930s Santa milk bottle wreath. This slid down the neck of your milk bottle to wish you 'Season's Greetings' from your friendly Borden's milkman, 8" tall x 7" wide. $45-50.

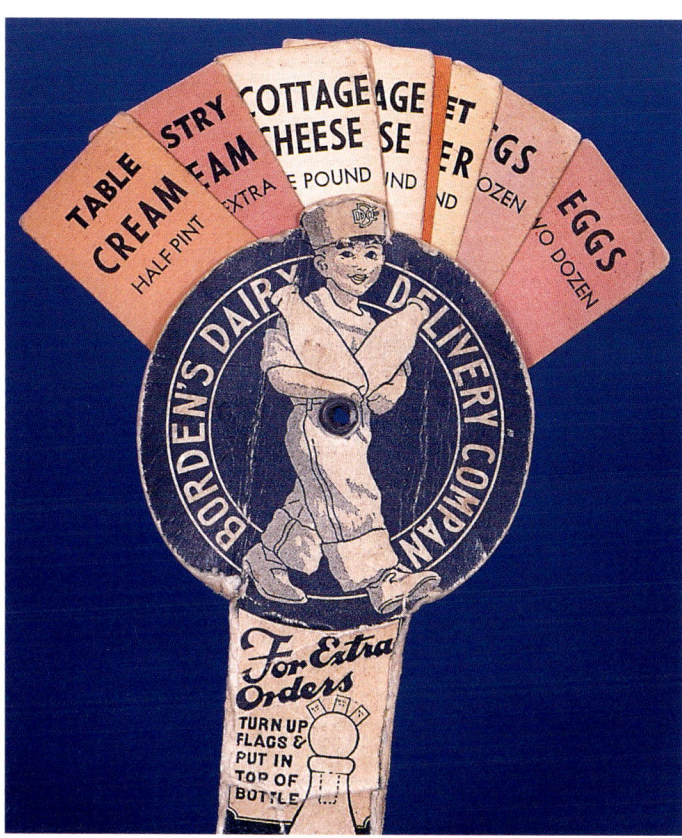

1930s indicator. The customer would turn up flags of desired products and insert bottom of indicator into an empty milk bottle. When the milkman picked up your empty bottles, he could see exactly what you needed that day, i.e., chocolate milk, cottage cheese, eggs, etc. $50-60.

1930s indicator. Used to let the milkman know what Borden's products you needed for that day and enabled you to place an order. $45-50.

Borden's juice bottles came in cool shapes. The two, one-quart bottles on either end go for $40-50, and the two, half-pint bottles are $25-30.

1930s-1940s flat-topped milk cartons. Checkerboard, one-pint size: $30-35; checkerboard, one-quart size: $40-45.

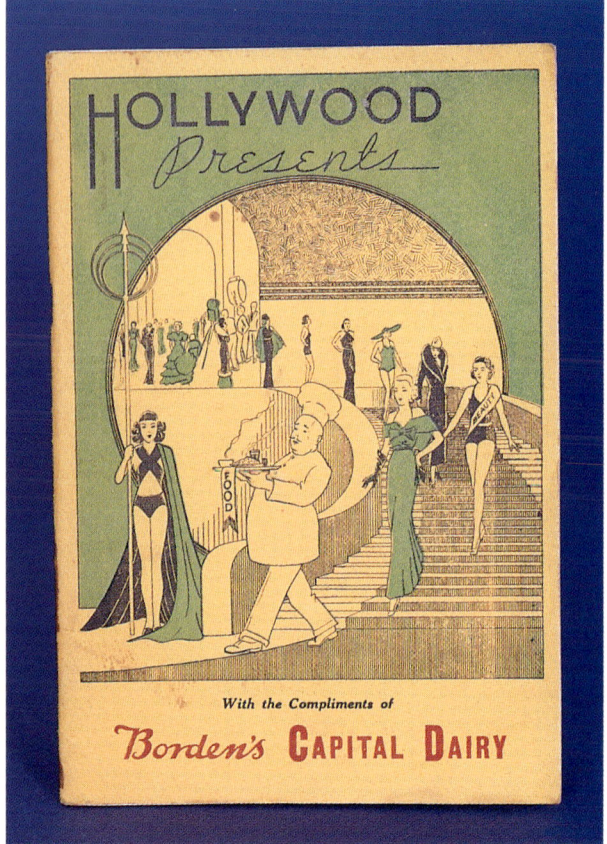

1930s promotional book filled with pictures of Hollywood movie stars. It includes recipes, fashion tips, and exercises for the women looking to keep their shapely figures. $35-40.

1940s deck of playing cards from Borden's Dairy Delivery Co., San Francisco, CA. $35-40.

1937 set of four one-quart milk bottles celebrating Borden's 80th Anniversary.
Cream-tops: $85-90 each; standard quart: $70-75 each.

1937-1939 Borden's began using cow characters in their promotions. Pictured here on
cheese spread jars (later used as juice glasses when you were finished with the product)
are Baby Beulah, Aunt Elsie, and Celestine. 3.5" tall. $35-40 each.

Beulah Borden comic book with Bossie as a lead character, no where mentioning Beulah or Elsie??? Book includes dairy techniques followed by Borden's to assure that the highest standards were set for their products, 6" x 4.5". $50-60.

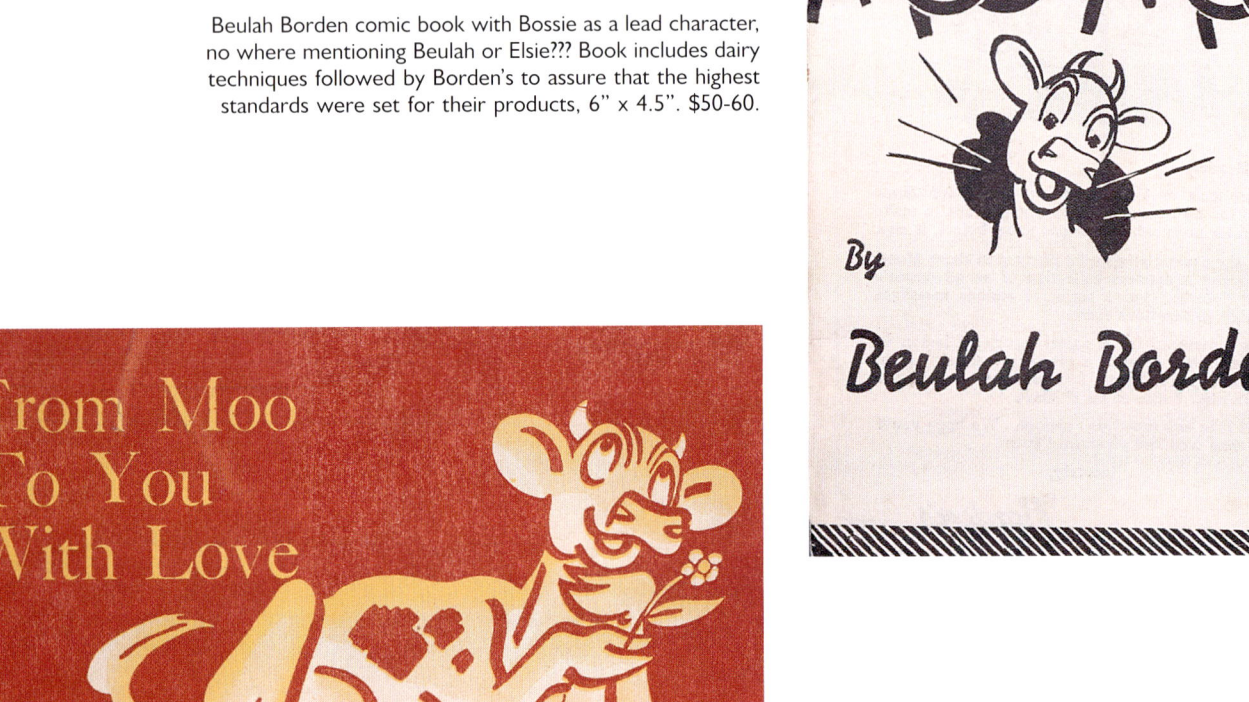

1937-1939 Borden's comic book featuring an early Elsie character, 6.75" x 4.5". $50-60.

Same comic book, now opened, shows Bossie the cow as Elsie's daughter (later to be dropped from the family when the 1939 World's Fair opened). $50-60.

FOUR STAR
FOUNTAIN SERVICE
Borden's
ICE CREAM
COPYRIGHT 1938 BY THE BORDEN COMPANY

Borden's, double-sided, porcelain 'Four Star Fountain Service' sign, dated 1938, 30" x 22". $400-450.

1930s Borden's ice cream paper plate, 6" x 6". $20-25.

Ink blotter from 1939 San Francisco Expo., 6" x 3". $20-25.

'Where's Elsie?' pin back button. Made when 60% of the public viewing the Borden's exhibit at the 1939 New York World's Fair wanted to know which cow was Elsie. $50-60.

Set of five postcards in the original envelope, designed by Walter Early. 1939-1940 Elsie takes her place as Borden's advertising icon. $125-150.

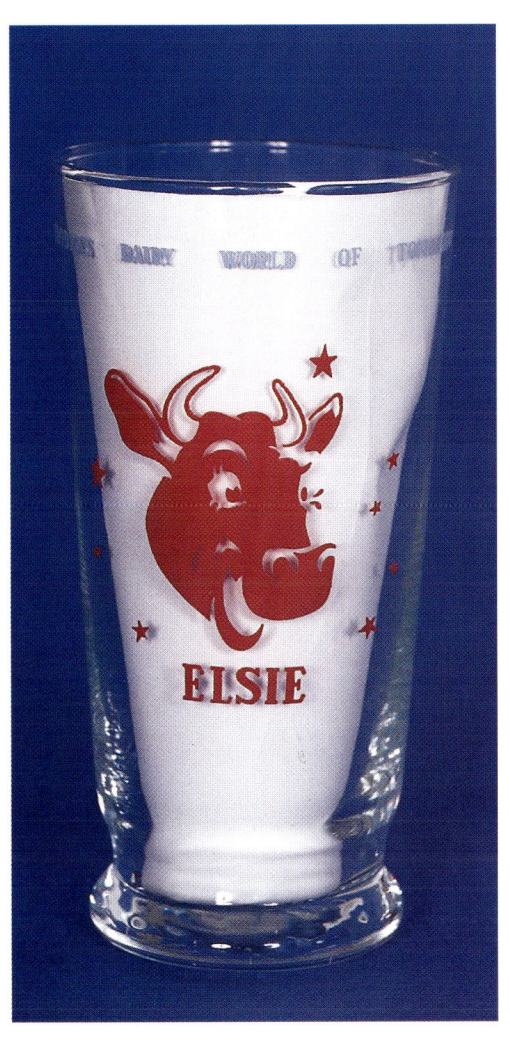

Elsie soda-fountain glass from 1939 New York World's Fair, 6" tall. Top reads 'Borden's Dairy World of Tomorrow.' $50-60.

1939 World's Fair cook book, 9" x 6.5". $25-30.

1940 Elsie souvenir ticket advertising the movie *Little Men* in which she made her film debut, 5.5" x 2". $45-50.

Chapter Two

Advertisement Signs, Items & Promotions

1939-1967

Like all major companies, Borden's promoted their products with clever slogans and eye-catching advertisements. After Elsie the Cow became Borden's famous advertising icon in 1939, the companies popularity grew more than ever before. Elmer, her husband, and their children, Beulah and Beauregard, also made an appearance in the promotion of Borden's products. Though Elsie's appearance changed throughout the years, her image remained synonymous with the high standards of the Borden's company. You could not go to a soda fountain, grocery store, or restaurant without seeing Elsie's friendly face promoting an array of Borden products—ice cream, milk, eggs, coffee and, yes, even dog food.

Beautiful set of four 1940s milk bottles portraying Elsie the Cow on the front. Cream-top: $125-135; standard quart: $85-95; pint: $45-50; half-pint: $30-35.

Display of 1950s restaurant creamers with various Borden's and
Elsie the Cow logos, difficult to find. $50-60 each.

Half-gallon milk bottles from the 1940s printed with two different Elsie logos.
$125-135.

Cream-top quart bottle with the now familiar Elsie
logo on the front, and on the back, a bold and
attractive advertisement for chocolate milk. $125-135.

1940s various shaped quart milk bottles with the familiar Elsie logo. Cream-tops: $125-135; standard quarts: $85-95.

These three one-quart bottles carry different Elsie logos on the back, but the fronts of the bottles all read 'Borden's Dairy Delivery Co.,' San Francisco, CA. Cream-tops: $125-135; standard quart: $85-95.

Rare and hard to find, wide-mouth gallon milk bottles with Elsie the Cow. $450-500.

Square milk bottles with two versions of the Elsie logo used in the 1950s. Square gallon, $65-70. Half-gallon, $30-35. Quart, $20-25.

Four amber-colored milk bottles from the 1950s. These amber bottles were made to help protect the vitamins in the milk from the sunlight. Square gallon, $50-60. Two half-gallons, $35-40 each. Small half-pint, which is rare, $50-60.

1950s porch boxes were used to help keep your milk cold when the milkman made his deliveries to your door step. $100-125 each.

Early 1940s Elsie the Cow indicator, used to place your order with the milkman. $75-85.

Late 1940s indicator, used to place your order with the milkman. $75-85.

41

Late 1940s Gail Borden and
Elsie the Cow indicator. $65-75.

1950's Elsie the Cow indicator. Daisy design
was added to the Elsie logo in 1951. $65-75.

Late 1940s Christmas bottle wreath, made of paper, 7" tall. $50-60.

Late 1940s vibrant paper Christmas wreath, used to wish customers 'A Merry Christmas and Happy New Year' from your friendly Borden's milkman, 10" tall. $50-60.

1950s paper Christmas wreaths, 5.5" tall, also found around the neck of milk bottles during the holiday season. $40-45 each.

Late 1950s Borden's paper milk carton bag, 8" tall. 'Very Big On Flavor' was the slogan during this era. $35-40. The three flat-top cartons pictured are from the late 1940s. Quarts sell for $45-50. Half-pint, $20-25.

Borden's salad dressing jars from the 1950s, 6" tall. $25-30 each.

Yes, Borden's was in the coffee business. These 1950s coffee jars are some of our favorites. The trial size jar, half-ounce jar, two-ounce jar, and five-ounce jar are valued at $20-25 each. The 'New Borden's Rich Roast,' unopened, $40-45. Red plastic coffee spoon with Elsie, $20-25.

Borden's Cottage Cheese containers from the 1950s. The large, five-pound containers, $40-45 each. The smaller, two-pound containers, $20-25 each.

Starlac powdered milk from the 1950s, boxes 6" tall. $30-35 each.

Malted milk one-pound tins with a variety of lithos, allowed you to have 'Soda Fountain
Magic with a spoon' at home. $40-45 each.

Early 1940s 2.5 gallon ice cream container, with older Elsie's face and their famous logo: "If It's Borden's It's Got To Be Good." $85-95.

Post-war 1945-1948 checkerboard pattern design, notice the changes in Elsie. 2.5 gallon ice cream container, $85-95.

Post-war store poster of Elsie and family in the kitchen, 30" x 44". $200-250.

Hand-painted and framed ice cream soda and milk shake soda fountain signs from the 1940s, 16" x 23". $65-75.

Double-sided, WWII Elsie display supporting the purchase of war bonds,
37" x 20". Elsie's new look here, attained in late 1941. $100-125.

1957 four wood framed soda fountain displays enticing the customer with pictures of milk shakes, banana splits, sundaes, and malts, all made with Borden's ice cream, 15" x 21". $65-75 each.

Set of four cardboard, stand-up soda fountain displays from the 1950s. Each one pictures a tempting ice cream treat. 18" tall. $100-125 each.

Cardboard, stand-up Elsie ice cream display from the 1950s, 18" tall. $65-75.

One Hundredth Year Anniversary, Elsie stand-up soda fountain display from 1957, 24" tall. $100-125. This design was used to celebrate Borden's one hundredth year in business and the coming of the 'Second 100 Years.'

Rare, 3-D Elsie, soda fountain, stand-up, cardboard display from 1957. Found mint in the box, 40" x 24" . $750-900.

Cool! Elsie 'Dessert Magic' ice cream display poster from the 1950s, 33" x 23". $100-125.

Late 1950s Elsie stand-up, cardboard ice cream carton display, 21" x 28". $275-300.

1950s Borden's half-gallon ice cream cartons. $40-45 each.

Borden's 1940s-1950s swoop design ice cream carton. $40-45.
Plastic ice cream scoop from the 1950s. $30-35.

Colorful Elsie ice cream pie container, from the late 1950s to early 1960s, 8"x 8". $40-45.

Elsie the Cow and her family in cardboard display form. These late 1940s displays were used in soda fountains and grocery stores, approximately 10" x 9". $125-150 each.

Tenth Anniversary Portrait from 1949, marks the tenth year celebration for Elsie the Cow as Borden's advertising icon. Cardboard, stand-up or wall display, 25" x 19". $250-300.

Cardboard shipping boxes, also used for advertisement of products in your local grocery store. The era ranges from 1940-1949, notice the changes in Elsie through the years. $50-60 each.

Store display poster, 42" x 29", 'Make Every Meal A Party.' $125-150.

Rare promotional poster advertising 'Freedomland,' an amusement park in New York that was built in the shape of the United States. Elsie had her own boudoir located at the park from 1960-1963 (park closed soon after) where you could visit her in person. Measures 44" x 27". $600-650.

Product headers from the late 1950s to early 1960s used in grocery stores, 32" x 20". $65-75.

'Borden's Fresh Ranch Eggs' carton. $45.

Plastic straws container, mid 1960s. $30-35.

Early 1950s 'Elsie Ice Cream' neon sign, 18" x 30". $600-650.

Late 1950s Elsie 'Borden's Ice Cream' neon sign, with daisy around Elsie. (Daisy design was added to Elsie in 1951.) 32" x 18". $600-650.

Mid 1950s Lady Borden neon sign, 19" x 34". Lady Borden was an ice cream specialty product by Borden's. $450-500.

1950s 'Borden 's Dairy Products' neon sign, 48" x 23". $450-500.

1950s 'Borden's Ice Cream' neon sign, 16" x 24". $400-450.

1950s 'Borden's Rich Milk' neon sign, 16" x 24". $400-450.

1950s 'Borden's Ice Cream' swoop design, 15" diameter, PAM clock (manufactured by PAM Clock Company Incorporated, New Rochelle, New York). Notice the curve in the colors of the clock and how they 'swoop' together. $500-600.

1950s 'Borden's Milk and Cream' swoop design, 15" diameter, PAM clock. $500-600.

Set of 1950s 'Borden's Ice Cream' and 'Borden's Fine Dairy Products,' 15" diameter, PAM clocks. $500-600 each.

Set of 1950s bright yellow 'Borden's Ice Cream' and 'Borden's Fine Dairy Products,' 15" diameter, PAM clocks. $500-600 each.

Mid 1950s Elsie daisy design, 15" diameter, PAM clocks. $500-600 each.

Late 1950s 'Very Big On Flavor,' 15"
diameter, PAM clock. $500-600.

Two 15" square clocks advertising 'Borden's Dairy Products' and 'Borden's Milk and
Cream.' $350-400 each.

1950s 'Borden's Ice Cream, Elsie Brand Specialties' clock with rotating Elsie disc on left side of sign, 36" x 13". $475-500.

'Borden's Ice Cream' light-up sign with clock, 47" x 11". $250-300.

1950s 'Lady Borden Ice Cream' light-up sign with clock, 30" x 14". $200-250.

Late 1950s 'Very Big On Flavor' ice cream sign and clock, 12" x 19". $200-250.

Early 1950s Elsie 'Milk and Cream' light-up spinner, with swoop design. There is a spinning motion around Elsie's head when lit. Animated and rare, $650-700.

70

Mid 1950s grocery store 'Ice Cream Department' light-up sign, 15" x 49". $375-400.

1950s Borden's 'Dairy Department' light-up sign, 26" x 15". In fair condition, $200-225.

Early to mid 1950s 'Dairy Department' light-up sign, 25" x 8". $300-350.

1950s 'Borden's Ice Cream' light-up sign, 24" x 8.5". $250-300.

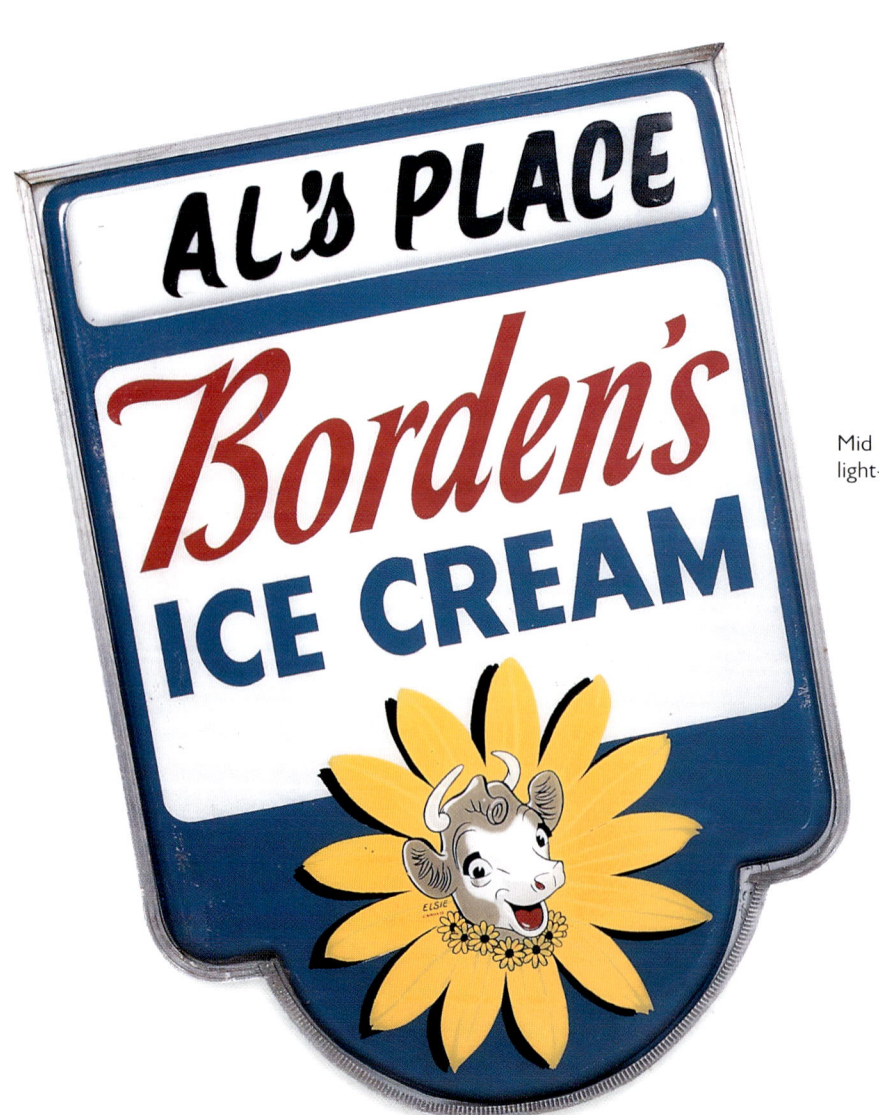

Mid 1950s Borden's dealer panel light-up sign, 4' x 3'. $450-500.

Large 1950s Borden's light-up sign, 47" x 18". $275-300.

1950s Borden's ice cream 'Just Has To Be Good' light-up sign, 24" x 18." $275-300.

Late 1950s 'Very Big on Flavor' ice cream light-up sign, 24" x 13". $275-300.

Borden's 1950s ice cream sign, 29" x 18". $225-250. One-quart ice cream carton, on the left, $35-40. One-pint carton, on the right, $25-30.

1950s 'Borden's Ice Cream' double sided sidewalk sign on stand, 28" x 20". $500-550.

Nice looking, metal Elsie milk carton display sign, 10" x 7". $175-200.

A large and colorful ice cream sign was a common sight outside many grocery stores in the 1950s, 6' x 2'. $275-300.

That 's right—Borden's also made dog food. This sign dates back to the 1950s, 20" x 14". $400-450. The dog food bag valued at $30-35.

Metal ice cream sign from the mid 1950s, 28" x 20". $225-250.

Metal 'Borden's Milk and Cream' signs, like this one, hung on the side of Borden's delivery trucks in the mid to late 1950s, 44" x 24". $250-300.

Attractive, 39" button style 'Borden's Ice Cream' sign, mid 1950s. $375-400.

Metallic blue, 34" 'Borden's Ice Cream' sign, late 1950s. $375-400.

Metallic blue, 24" 'Borden's Ice Cream' sign, late 1950s. $275-300.

The most familiar sign that Borden's produced, Elsie with a yellow daisy background, 24" die-cut. $275-300. The quart, flat-top milk cartons are valued at $30-35. The half-pints, $20-25.

Borden's milk carton sign, difficult to find, 47" x 22". $400-475.

34" die-cut, Elsie daisy sign. $375-400.

Borden's 'Open/Close' sign,
14" x 9". $300-350.

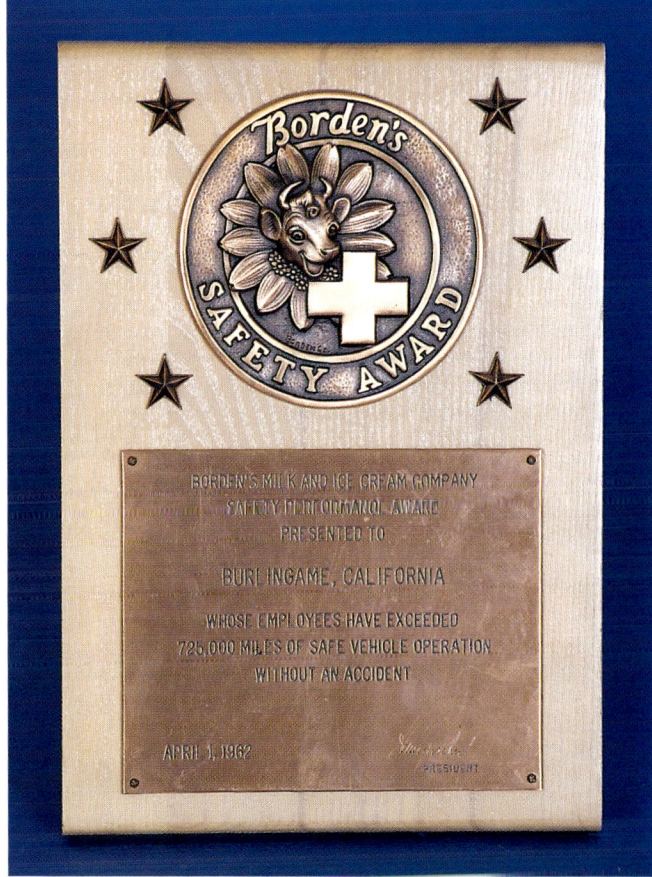

Borden's Safety Award plaque, issued to Burlingame,
California Plant for safe vehicle operation, dated 1962,
9" x 12.5". $250-275.

27" x 8" wall thermometer, $275-300. Half-gallon ice cream carton, on the left,
$35-40. One-quart carton, on the right , $25-30.

A variety of menu boards, from the mid 1950s to the late 1950s. Given to soda fountains to list the many flavors of Borden's ice cream from which customers could choose. $175-200.

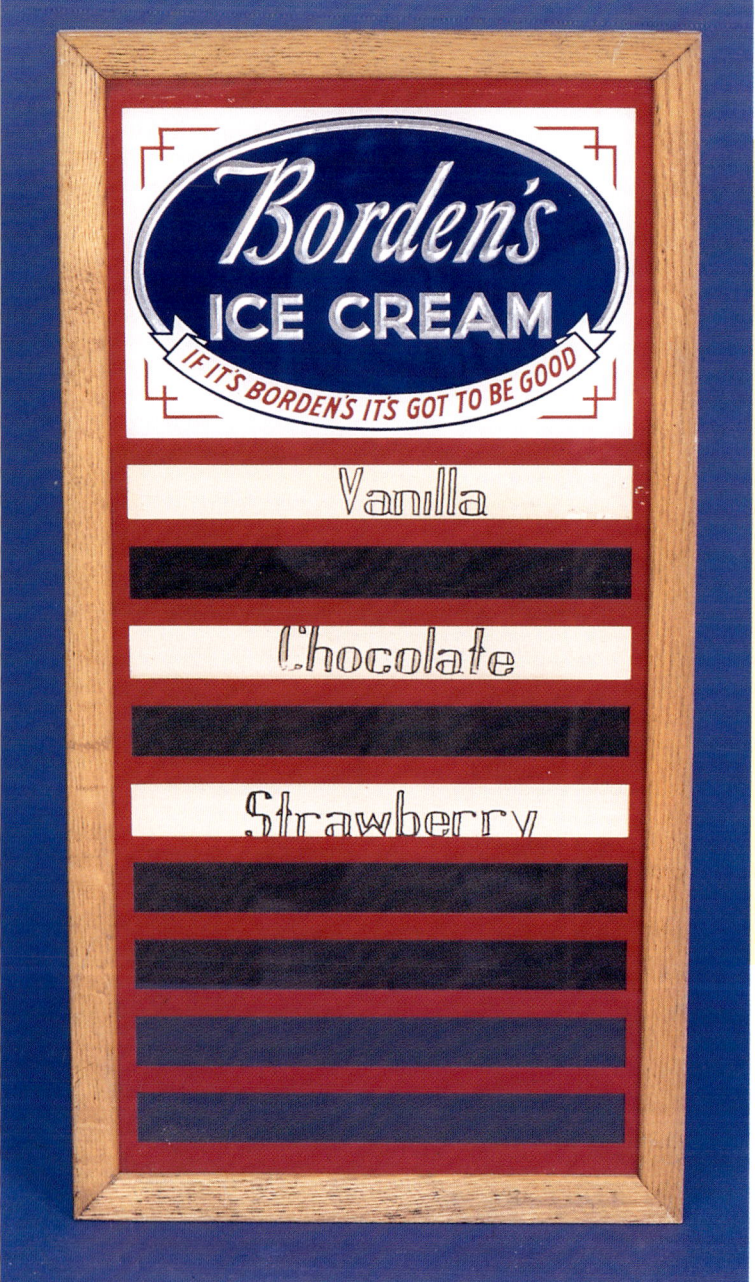

Stand-up menu board, made of cardboard, early 1960s, 24" x 14". $100-125.

Chapter Three
Promotional Items & Related Collectibles

1939-1967

Being a major company in the consumer market, Borden's manufactured many promotional items and related collectibles (known to collectors as "go-withs") to encourage the growth and popularity of their products. Having Elsie the Cow and her family on their side, the possibilities were endless. Toys, games, chinaware, pottery, lighters, and jewelry were just a few of the items that Borden's had produced using pictures and graphics of Elsie and her popular family. Some of the most creative and imaginative ideas were used to help keep Borden's a common household name for years to come—and to keep collectors, like ourselves, searching for it all!

1939 pamphlet on the many uses and recipe suggestions for Borden's Chateau, 'The Aristocrat of Cheese Foods.' $10-15.

1940 Elsie the Cow cookbook containing recipes that used Borden's Eagle Brand Milk. $25-30.

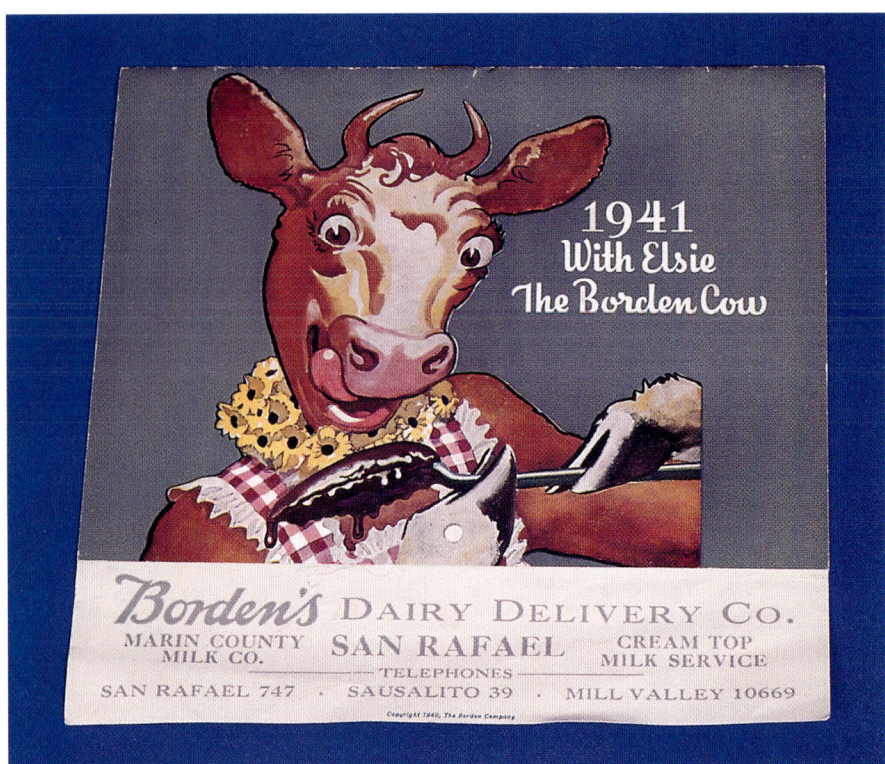

1941 Borden's Dairy Delivery calendar with early Elsie. Never used and in mint condition, $90-100.

1941 *Borden's Cheese Sales Manual*, 8.5" x 5". $40-45.

1941 promotional comic lithos, six in the original envelope, 7.5" x 7". $100-125.

1941 Borden's ordering card for customers convenience in ordering extra dairy products, just mark the amount of product needed and hang around your empty milk bottle. $25-30.

1941 *Borden's Cartoon Book*, 3" x 4", given to customers compliments of 'Elsie the Borden Cow.' $25-30.

1948 *Milk Goes To Town* story book, featuring Elsie and Beauregard on the front cover and Elmer and Beulah on the back, 6" x 4". $40-45.

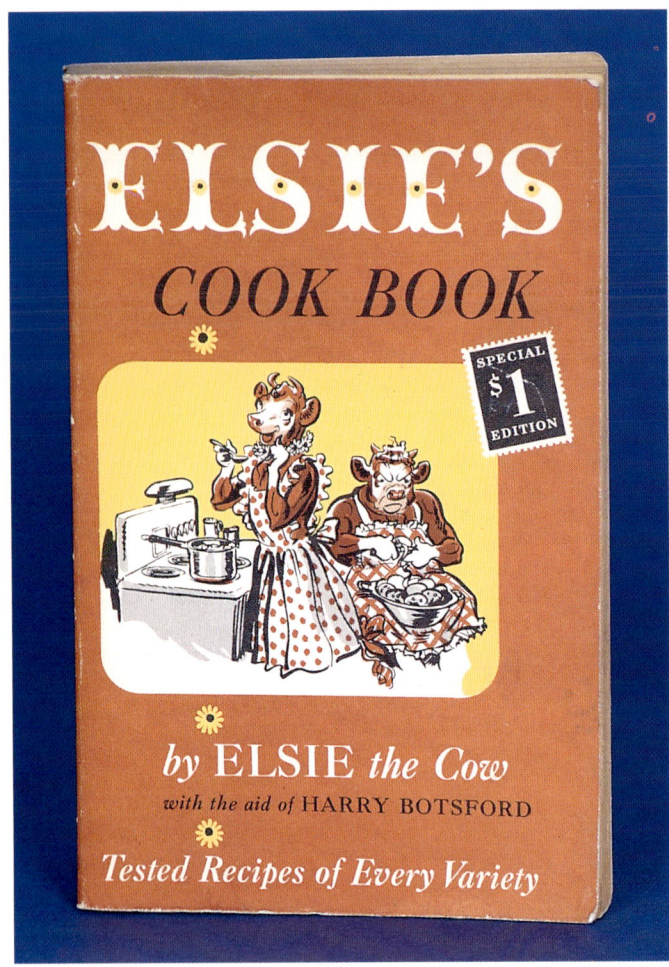

Elsie's Cook Book, dated 1952, soft-cover with 374 pages. $40-45.

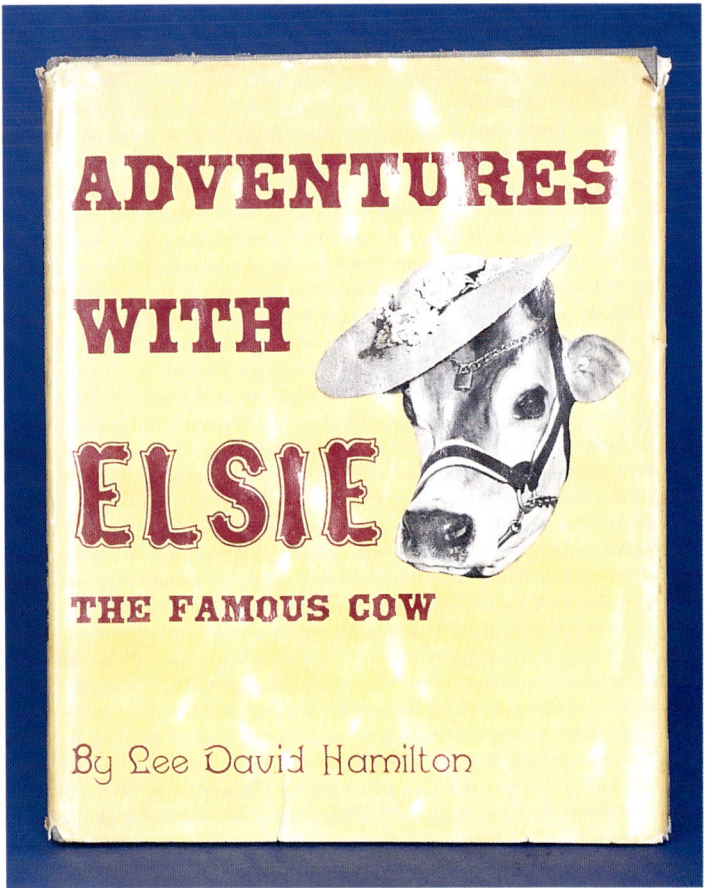

Adventures with Elsie, the Famous Cow. This book is dated 1964 and tells the story of Elsie from 1939 to 1964. $40-45.

Five 1950s Elsie comic books for boys and girls. $40-45 each.

Pop-up Christmas cards with Elsie and her family. They have great detail and graphics, 1940s-1950s. $45-50 each.

from Elsie, Elmer,
Beulah, Beauregard
and
M. Strawbecker

Ink blotters with wonderful graphics of Elsie and her family, 1940s era. $35-40 each.

Menu holders for holding soda fountain or restaurant menus at your table, 3.5" diameter, 1950s. $100-125 each.

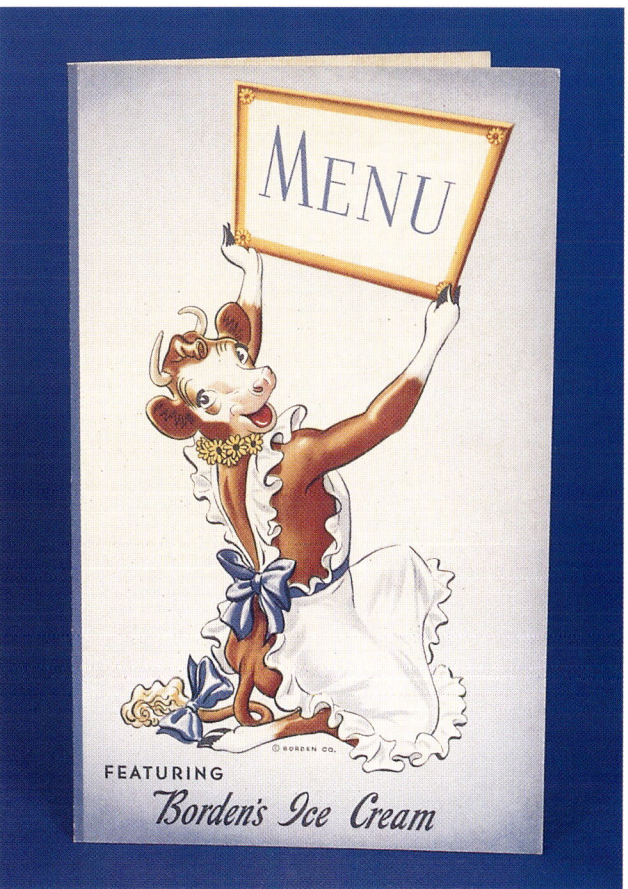

From Moo To You, starring Elsie is a "teacher's guide to an educational picture on Milk." This 1941 book came with a nine-minute educational film on the production and value of milk. $100-125. (I have never been able to find this film, but I will!!!)

Late 1940s Elsie menu cover, used in restaurants or diners, 9.5" x 6". $35-40.

Two 1950s Elsie calendars. In fair condition, $40-50.

Bordenews and *Elsie's Horn* were newsletters for company employees and stockholders, containing information on the employees in their specific divisions, i.e., safety awards, marriages, births, Elsie's visits and honors, and credit union issues. $30-35 each.

Paper megaphones (unwaxed never used as milk containers), giveaways at local sports events. We believe they were filled with popcorn. $65-75 each.

Elsie's Good Food Line Train, premium cut-out sheet on litho paper from the mid 1950s, uncut, 37" x 27.5". $125-150.

Borden's hosiery mending kits from the 1940s and 1950s. $20-25 each.

Elsie also knew how to fish. Here is *How To Tie Knots*, a fishing booklet from the 1940s, 4.5" x 3". $25-30.

1957 Centennial Dinner program, a Centennial ribbon with name tag, and a Centennial napkin—all from the Centennial Kick-Off Program and Dinner, January 5, 1957, in San Jose, CA., which celebrated Borden's One-Hundredth Anniversary. Ribbon, $25-30. Dinner program, $20-25. Napkin, $10-15.

1950s Borden's paper hats worn inside the milk plants by employees. $20-25 each.

Make Elsie smile cardboard game. You try to make a smiling face for Elsie out of the little chain as you tap on the back of the card. From the mid 1940s. $70-75.

1941 Elsie the Cow tin-ring puzzle game. "Elsie, the Borden cow is no puzzle to her pals" states the litho. Object of this game is to get all six rings around Elsie's horns. 3.5" x 2.5". $175-200.

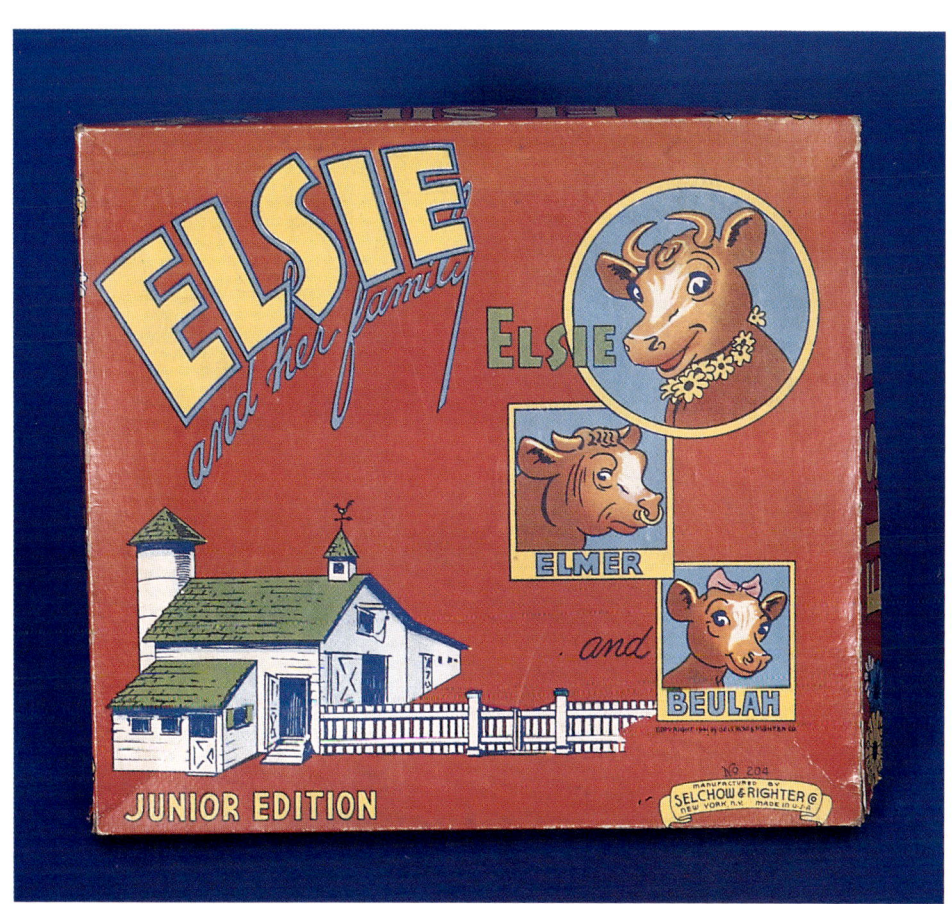

No. 204, 1941 'Elsie and her Family' board game, junior edition. Manufactured by Selchow and Righter Co., NY. $75-95.

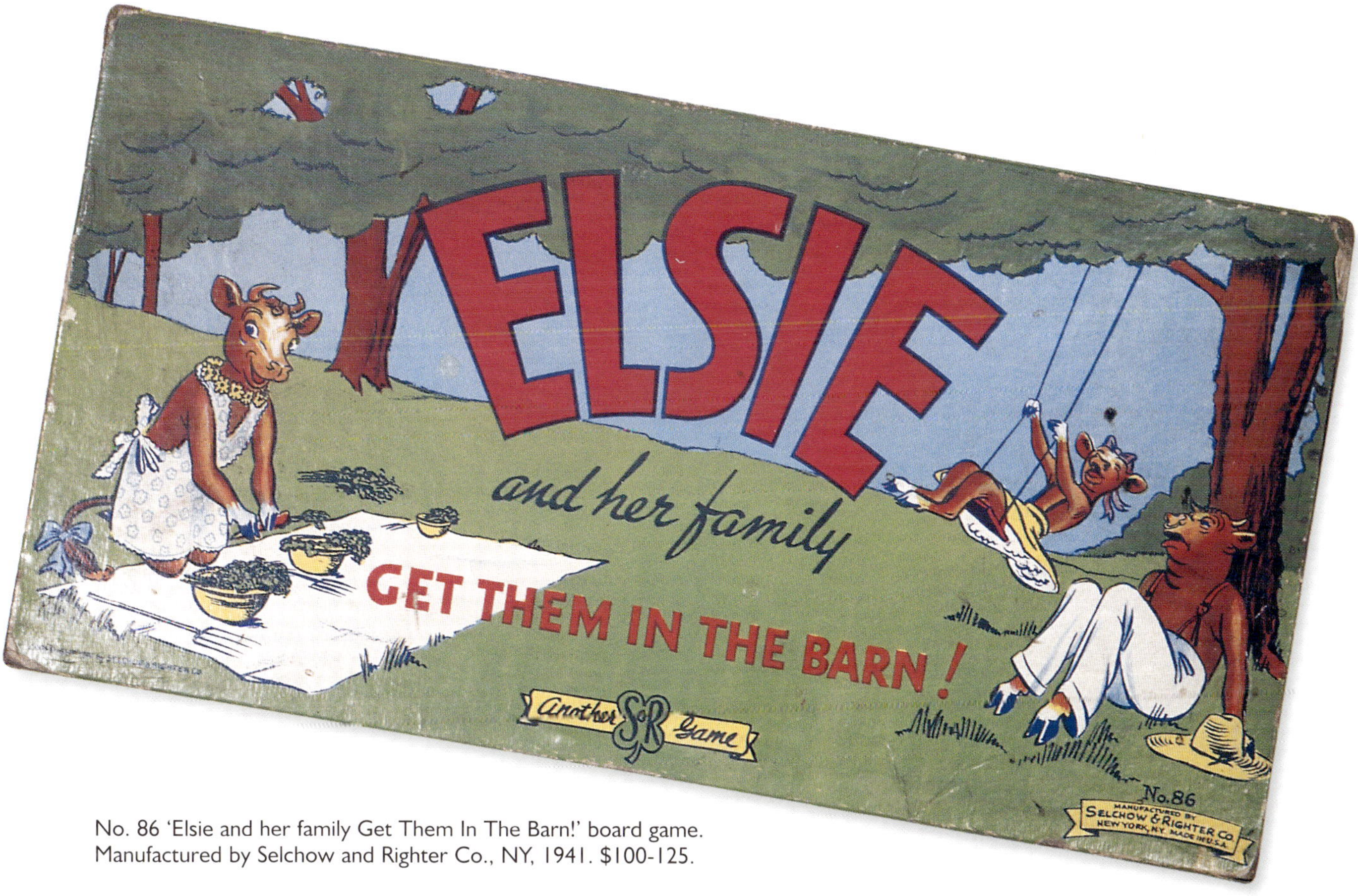

No. 86 'Elsie and her family Get Them In The Barn!' board game. Manufactured by Selchow and Righter Co., NY, 1941. $100-125.

Board game No. 86, 'The Elsie Game,' with Elsie, Elmer, and Beulah. Manufactured by Selchow and Righter Co., NY, mid 1940s-1950s. $90-100.

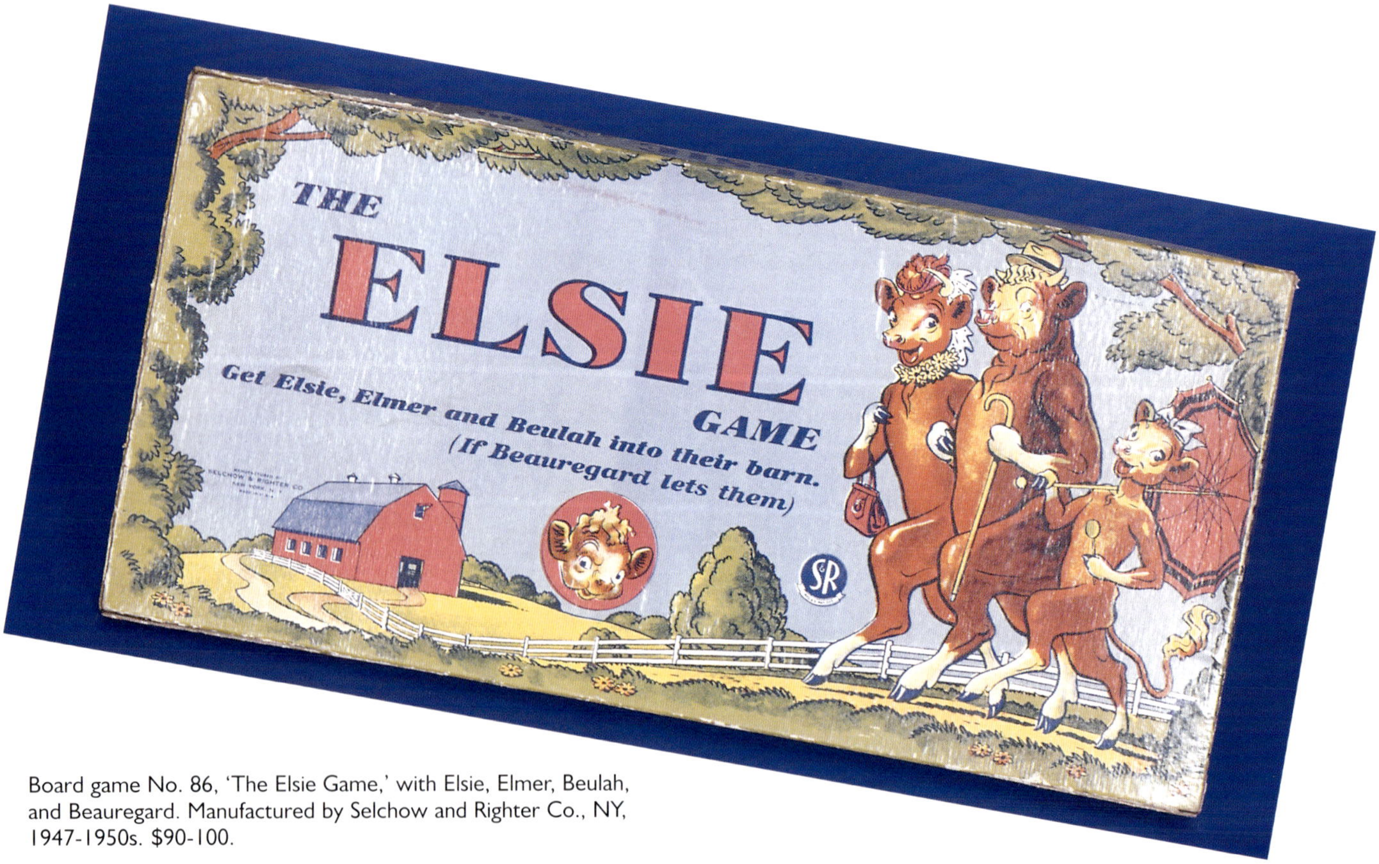

Board game No. 86, 'The Elsie Game,' with Elsie, Elmer, Beulah, and Beauregard. Manufactured by Selchow and Righter Co., NY, 1947-1950s. $90-100.

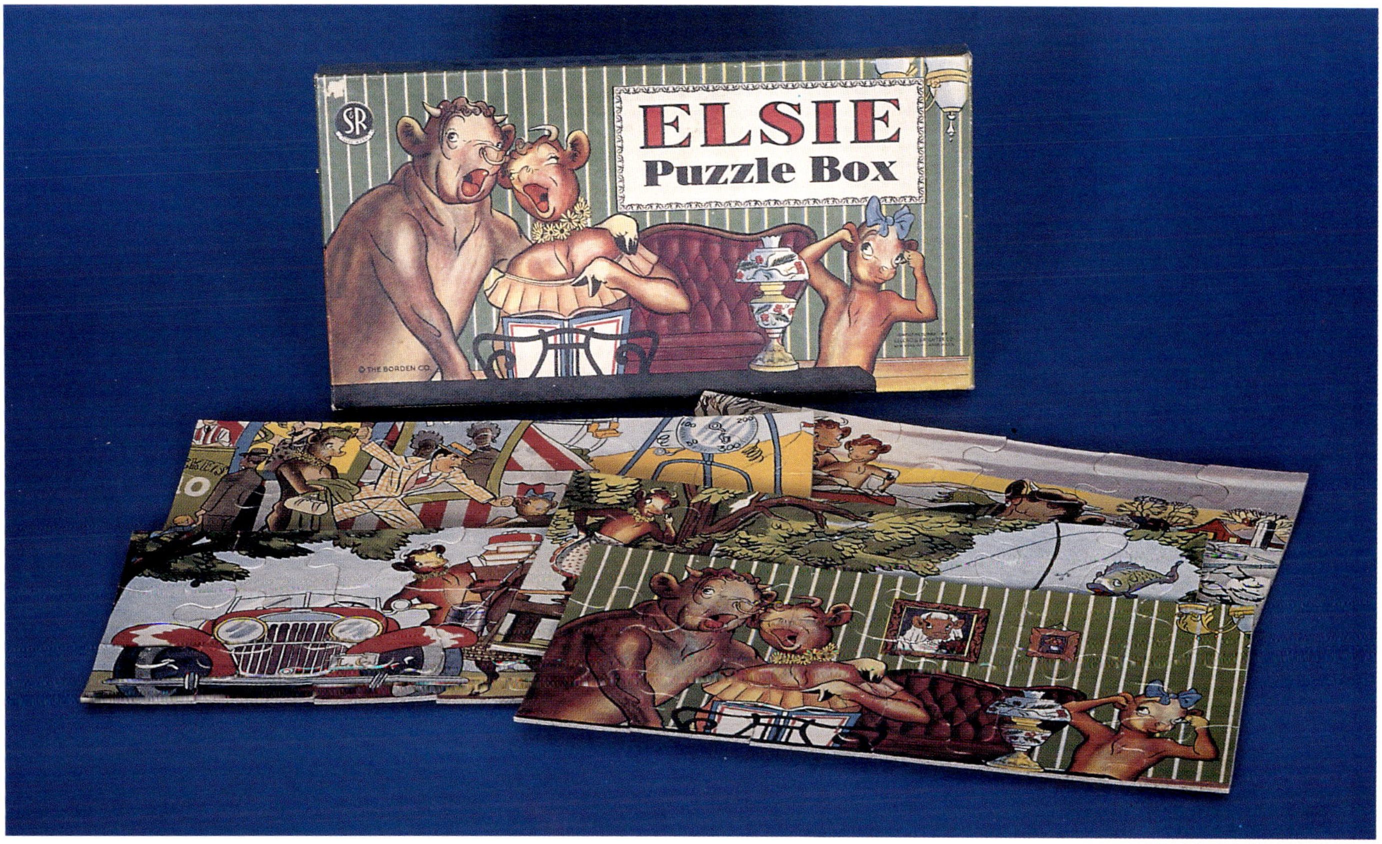

No. 501 Elsie puzzle box, five complete puzzles, manufactured by Selchow and Righter Co., NY, late 1940s-1950s. $150-175.

Dated 1958, No. 140, 'Elsie's Ice Cream Cone Pop Game,' Wilkening Manufacturing Co., PA. $75-95.

Early 1950s Elsie and family glasses, brown and yellow, 4.75 " tall. $75-85 each.

Early 1940s, Elsie, Elmer, and Beulah glass, 4.5" tall. Poem on the back reads: "The Grass Is Green That Elsie Eats, For Milk That She'll Provide Us, And Creamy Milk Makes Ruddy Cheeks, After It Gets Inside Us." $75-95.

1963 'Elsie's Milkman Game,' manufactured by Smith-Edwards Co. $75-95.

Beulah and Beauregard glasses, 5" tall. $50-60 each.

White, Elsie milkshake glasses, 5" and 6" tall. 1950 era. $35-40 each.

Bright red, Elsie milkshake glasses, 6" and 5" tall, 1950s era. $50-60 each.

Cool set of graphics on these four glasses from the 1950s with Elsie and her family, approximately 5" tall. $75-95 each.

1950s Elsie measuring glass, 4.5" tall. $125-150.

Blue, highlighted Elsie glass, mid 1950s, approximately 5" tall. $65-75.

Borden's diner glasses, approximately 4" tall. $35-40 each.

Early 1960s Elsie glass, 5.5" tall. $35-40.

Baby warming dish, 8" diameter, stamped Juvenile Ware, made in the U.S.A. $250-275.

1940s Dancing Elsie children's set, stamped Juvenile Ware, made in the U.S.A.
Cup 3" tall, plate 7" in diameter, and bowl 5" in diameter. Set, $300.

1940s Elsie and Elmer coffee mugs, older design. Elsie mug, 2.5" tall, blue trim, stamped Juvenile Ware, made in the U.S.A. $50-55. Elmer mug, 3" tall, gold trim, marked The Borden Co. $50-55.

Punch bowl set featuring Elsie's family. Bowl, 10" in diameter; cups, 3" tall. Set, $750-800. Bowl only, $400-450.

Elsie, Elmer, Beulah, and Beauregard, set of four mugs
with original boxes, 3" tall. With boxes, $125-150 each;
without boxes, $65-75 each.

105

1950s raised Elsie mug with bell, 3.5" tall. Made by Cress Ceramics. $95-110.

1960s raised Elsie mug with bell, 3.5" tall. Bottom marked 'Made In Japan' and 'The Borden Company Limited.' $95-110.

1950s Elsie mug, 3.5" tall. Elsie is also on the inside bottom. $75-80.

Children's tin Elsie feeding cup, 1950s. $65-75.

Two Elsie and Elmer salt and pepper sets, 4" tall. Set on the left is unglazed and is valued at $150-175. Set on the right is glazed and valued at $100-125.

1950s Elsie stacked salt and pepper sets, 4" tall. Her head holds the pepper and her shoulders hold the salt. The white set with the Elsie label is valued at $100-125. Cream colored set, $75-80.

1950s Elsie full-body creamer, 4" tall. $100-125.

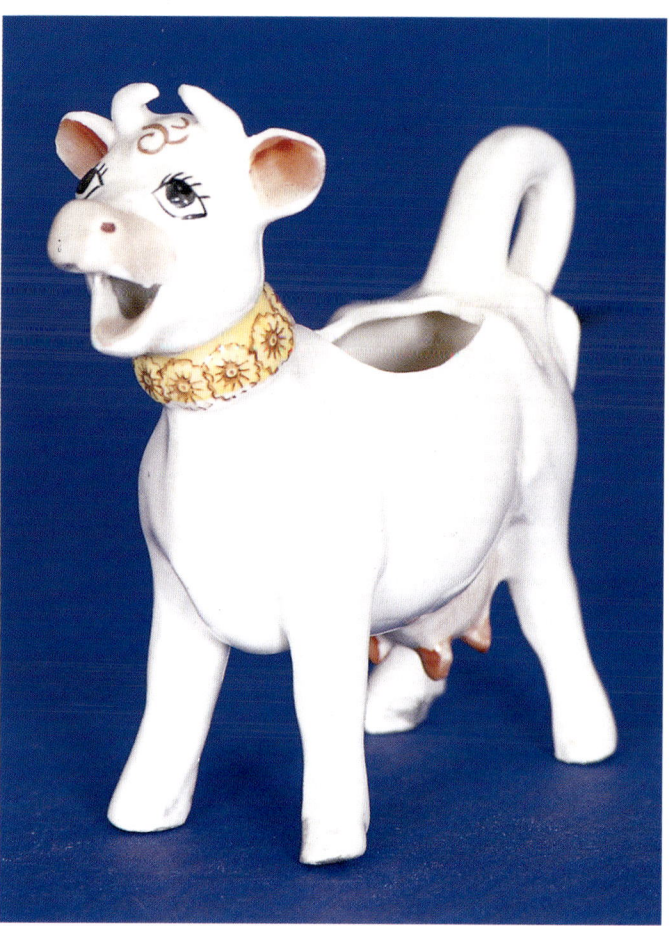

Late 1950s white Elsie full-body creamer, 4" tall. $100-125.

Light-brown Elsie and Elmer creamer and sugar set from the 1950s. $225-250.

Dark-brown Elsie and Elmer creamer and sugar set from the 1950s. $200-255.

1950s Beulah cookie jar that moos when you remove the lid, 11" tall. $350-375.

1950s Elsie the Cow cookie jar made by Pottery Guild of America. Elsie is 12" tall. $350-375.

Rare, 1940s Elsie the Cow glazed chalk lamp, 12" tall. Without original shade, $450-500.

Rare, 1940s Elmer glazed chalk lamp, 12" tall. Without original shade, $450-500.

Late 1940s to early 1950s Elsie and Beauregard rocking chair lamp with the very rare, original shade. Lamp, 12" tall without shade, $300-325. Original shade (alone), $600-650.

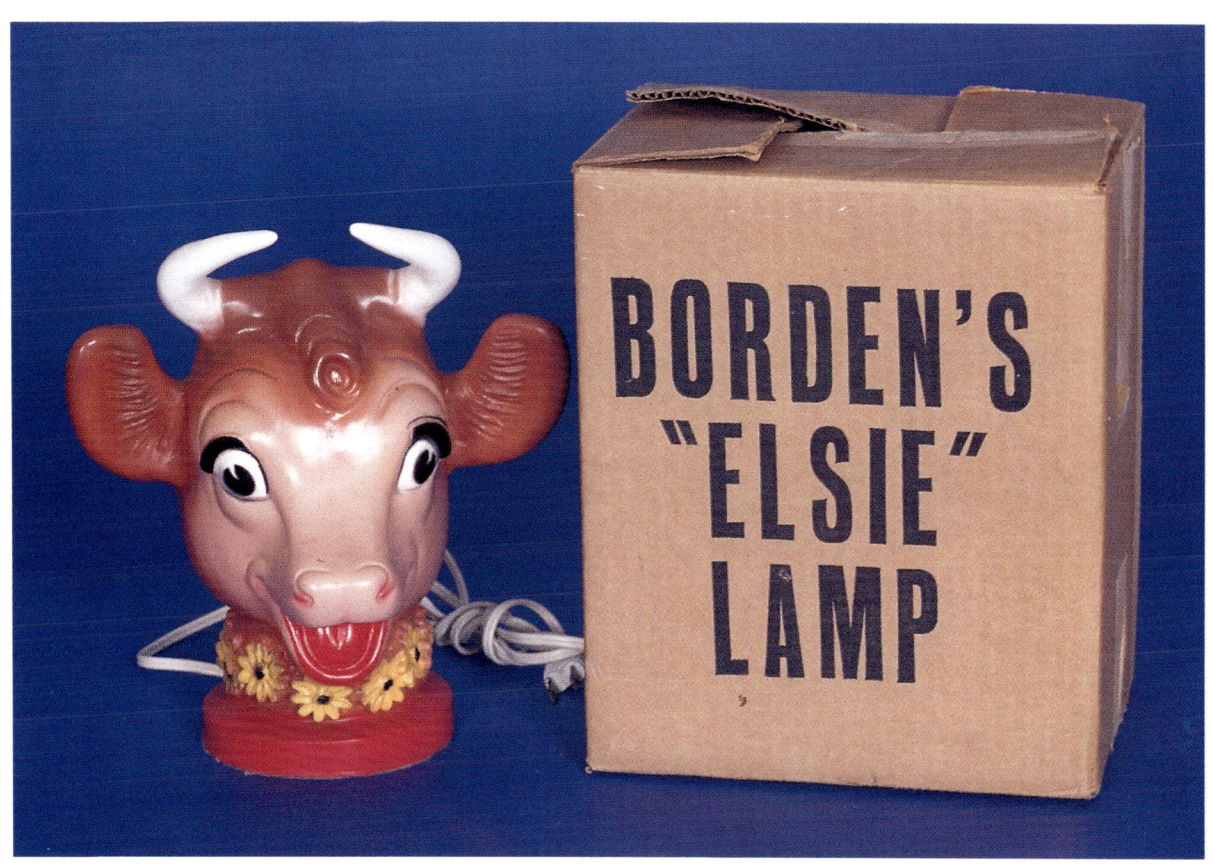

Late 1950s, early 1960s Elsie light-up head lamp, 10" tall, made of hard plastic.
With original box, $450-475. Lamp only, $350-375.

1950s Elsie eight-piece diner set, made by Wallace China, Los Angeles, CA.
This set is very hard to find. Single pieces sell for $75-100 each.

1960s cutting board for cheese with an Elsie tile, 18" x 6.5". $75-100.

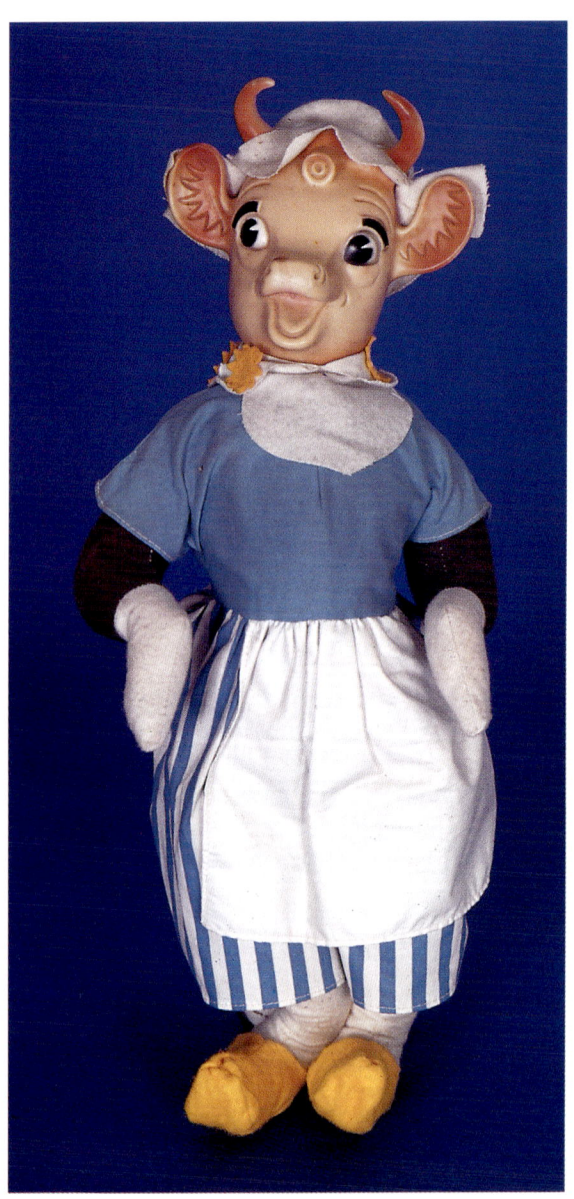

1940s Elsie 14" stuffed doll. This doll has great detail and is hard to find. $450-500.

1950s Elsie Dutch Chocolate doll, stands 21" tall. She was found in her original box. Borden's made a product called 'Borden's Dutch Chocolate' in the 1950s and 1960s. This doll was a promotion for this product. With box, $375-400. Doll only, $275-300.

114

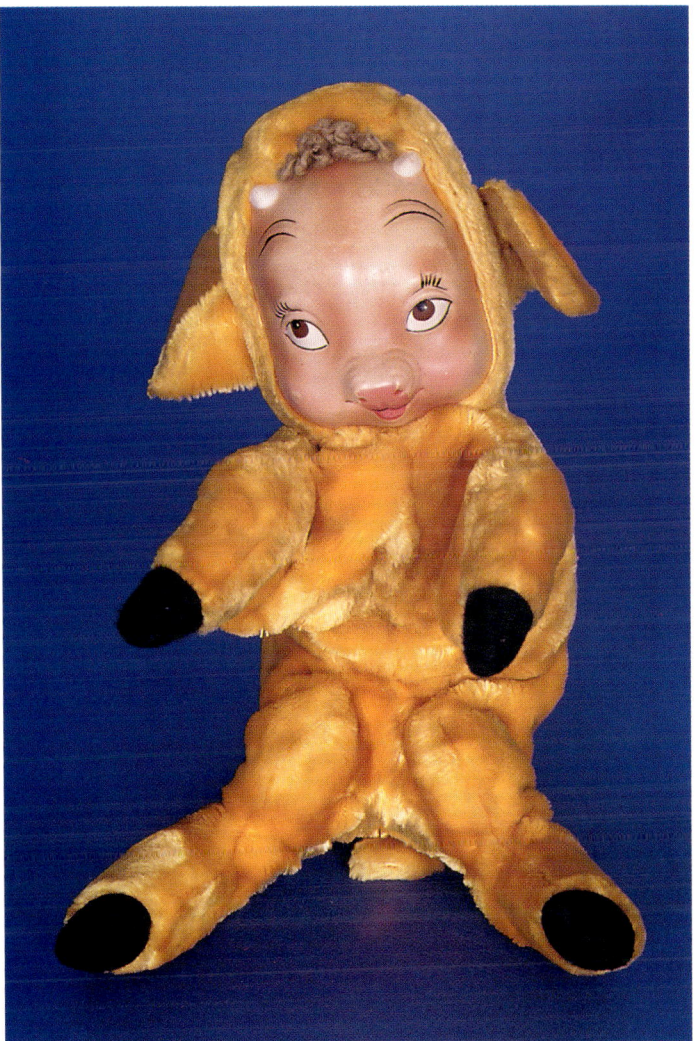

1950s Elsie the Cow dolls made by 'My-Toy Creation.' They are 13" tall and "moo" when you tip them. They are plush dolls with a soft rubber face. They came in blue, pink, and brown colors. $75-85 each.

Beauregard, 15", soft plush pajama doll made in the 1940s to 1950s. These dolls have celluloid, hand painted faces and a zipper on the back to put your pajamas in. They came in gold for the boys, and pink for the girls. $285-300.

1957 'Name Elsie's Twins' entry blank, 8" x 4". Contest was a promotion to help celebrate Borden's 100th Year in business and the birth of the new calves. $20-25.

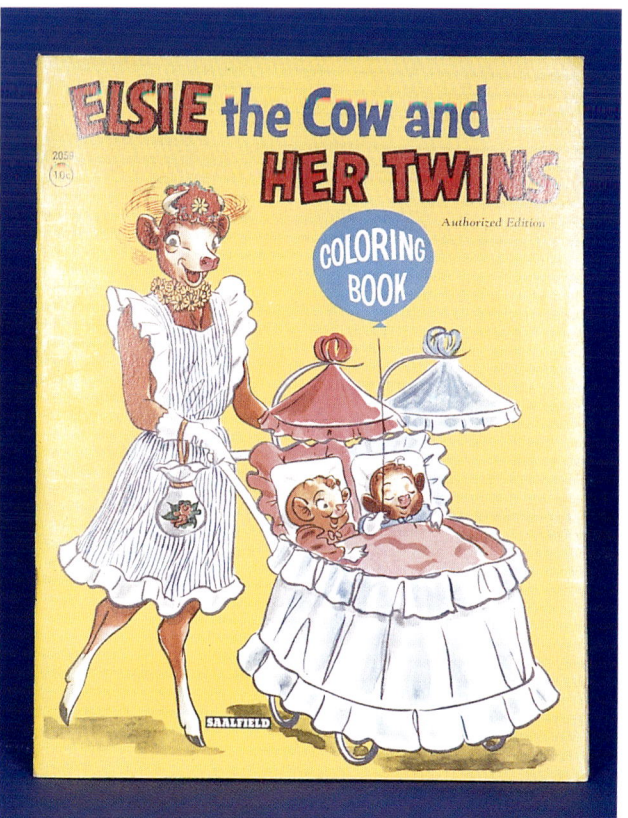

1957 *Elsie the Cow and Her Twins* coloring book, published by The Saalfield Publishing Co. A Borden's promotion celebrating their One Hundredth Year Anniversary. The twins were born and named Larabee and Lobelia. $25-30.

'My-Toy Creations' plush twin dolls, Larabee and Lobelia, 7" tall, produced in 1957. $100-125 each.

Elsie's twins, Larabee and Lobelia, hand-puppets by 'My-Toy Creations,' 8.5" tall, dated 1957. $95-100.

1944 Elsie pull toy. Box states "Elsie as the Cow Who Jumped Over the Moon," 10" tall x 7" long, made by Wood Commodities Corp., NY. With box, $450-500. Toy only, $300-350.

745 'Elsie's Dairy' truck, Fisher Price pull toy, driven by Beauregard. It originally came with two glass miniature milk bottles. 10" long x 7" tall, made in 1948. $450-500.

1960s friction, tin Borden's milk van, made in Japan, 8" long. $150-175.

Metal Buddy L 1960s Borden's milk van with plastic milk bottle carrier, 11" long. Milk bottle carrier originally came with plastic milk bottles. $250-275.

1960s plastic, 4" long, friction Borden milk van made by Gordy Mite . $45-50.

Die-cast, 2" long Borden's milk van. $30-35.

1940s Elsie and Beauregard wooden milk bucket, 6" tall. $150-175.

1940s Elsie push toy, 'The Tricky Cow That Moos.' When you push the button on the bottom, Elsie collapses and moos. Made by Mespo Products, 5" tall. With box, $200-225. Without box, $100-125.

Late 1940s brown Elsie cheese promotion vinyl box. These boxes were filled with
Borden cheeses and given as gifts. 11" x 14". Very hard to find, $225-250.

Late 1940s green Elsie cheese promotion
vinyl box, 12" x 9". $100-125.

Late 1940s red Elsie cheese promotion
vinyl box, 12" x 8". $75-100.

Late 1940s Elsie molded soap made by Lightfoot, 4" tall. With original box, $150-175. Soap only, $45-50.

Late 1940s Elsie molded soap made by Lightfoot, 5" tall. Value with original box, $150-175. Soap only, $75.

Late 1940s Beauregard molded soap made by Lightfoot, 5" tall with background display. Value with original box, $125-150. Soap with display, $65-75.

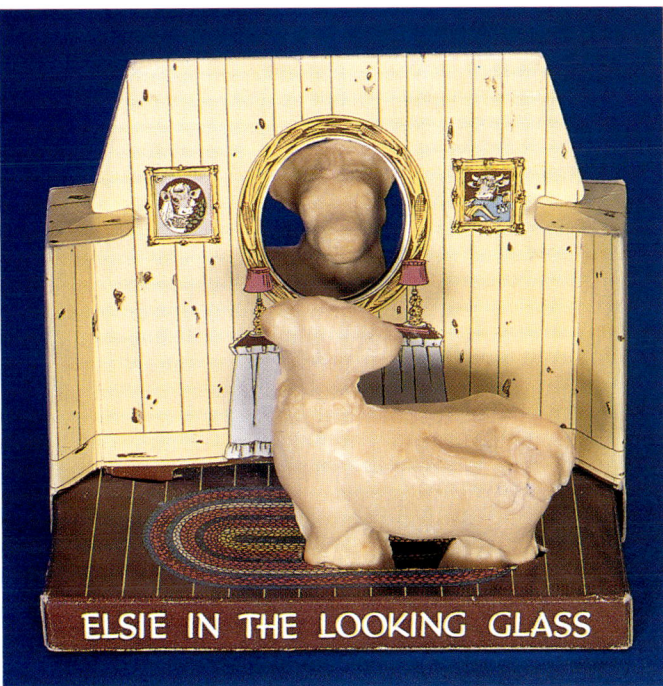

Late 1940s Elsie molded soap made by Lightfoot, 5.5" tall with background display. $75-100.

Late 1940s Elsie molded soap made by Lightfoot, 4.5" tall. $65-75.

Late 1940s framed Elsie and Family 3-D prints, illustrated by Walter Early. They measure 13.5" x 10.5". They look the same, but the one on the right glows in the dark. Print on the left, $100-125. Glow-in-the-dark print, $150-175.

Late 1940s framed Elsie and Family 3-D print, illustrated by Walter Early. Each print measures 13.5" x 10.5". $100-125 each.

124

Three, very rare, 1950s children's vinyl purses with plastic busts of Elsie and Beauregard. Black purse with Beauregard, 4" tall. Elsie purses, 5" tall. $175-200 each.

Late 1940s mixed set of Elsie's story book hankies, *Bringing up Elsie's Baby*, in four hanky chapters. Pictured is one story book with original, two blue hankies. Gray and pink hankies came together in another, very similar, version. Hankies measure 8" x 8". Hankies, $75-95 each. Book, $50-60.

1950s Beauregard pink rattle, 5" tall, made by Irwin. When you tip him back the milk in his bottle disappears. $100-125.

1950s Beauregard rocking rattle, 6.5", made by Irwin. Back side reads "Elsie's Baby Beauregard." $275-300.

1950s Beauregard rattle and squeaker, reads "Elsie's Baby Beauregard, press me." Very rare, 7.75" long, made by Irwin. $250-275.

1950s Beauregard banks in red and blue, 5" tall, made by Irwin. $65-75 each.

1950s Beauregard rattle and squeaker, reads 'Elsie's Baby Beauregard, press me,' also rare. 6.5" tall, made by Irwin. $300-350.

Extremely rare, 1950s Beauregard nodder, 7" tall. Front reads: 'Elsie's Baby Beauregard.' Made by Irwin. $450-500.

Beauregard child's feeding dishes from the 1950s, 7" tall. These are very rare. $450-500 each.

1940s Elsie and Beulah wooden war bond bank, 4.75"
tall. $100-125.

1940s Elsie pot-metal bank, made by Master Caster Mfg. Co.,
Chicago, 7" tall. $175-200.

1950s Elsie hard plastic bank, 10" tall. $300-350.

Elsie paper mask, 1940s, 11" x 12". $125-150.

1950s Elsie mask made of fabric (looks like cheesecloth), 11" x 10". $100-125.

1950s Elsie rubber squeeze toy, 5" tall, made by the Oak Rubber Co., Ohio. $75-100.

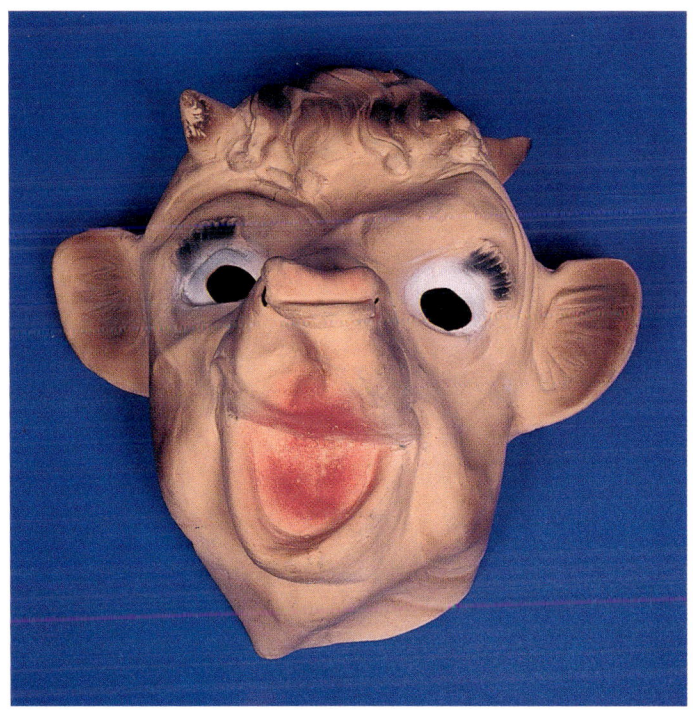

Elmer, late 1950s, rubber mask, made by Stone Rubber Toys Co., Connecticut, 9" x 8". $100-125.

1950s Children's Elsie and Elmer plastic creamer set, 3.5" tall. $150-175.

1950s Elsie and Beulah cookie cutters, approximately 2.5" in diameter. $45-50 each.

'Elsie's Milk Bottle' toy, dated 1956, by Royal Toy Co., Inc., NY, 6.5" tall. $100-125.

Elsie and Family Bar-B-Q tablecloth and apron, 1950s era. Tablecloth,
38" x 48". Tablecloth and apron, $100-125 each.

Elsie and Elmer Out West contains two 45 rpm records, by
London Records, dated 1950. $45-50.

Elmer, mid 1960s, glue containers. Left figural container is 6" tall and is valued at $60-75. The 4" container on the right is valued at $35.

Three Elsie balloons, 1950s, 7" deflated. $10-15 each.

1950s 'Elsie's Good Food Line' scarf, 19" x 19". $45-50.

Three sets of Elsie playing cards. The middle set is from the 1940s, $75-100 with original box. Each end set is from the 1950s, $45-50 each.

1950s Borden's patch and an Elsie patch from the same era. The Borden's patch is 10" long and is valued at $25-30. Elsie patch is 7" across and is valued at $30-35.

1950s Borden's patches. End patches measure 4" x 3"; middle patch is 5" x 4". $30-35 each.

1940s Elsie copper pin-back button, approximately 2" in diameter. $45-50.

1940s rare 'Elsie's Bagel & Cream Cheese Club' radio premium, pin-back button, 1.25" diameter. $150-200.

1940s war bond, 1.5", paper ribbon with plastic Elsie. $45-50.

Elsie, Beauregard, and Elmer 1940s, plastic, 2" tall pins. $ 45-50 each.

Elsie pin-back button from the 1940s, 75" diameter. $20-25.

1948 Elsie, 2" diameter, pin-back button. $45-50.

1950s soda fountain name tag, pin back, 2.5" x 1.5". $65-75.

1950s soda fountain name tag, pin back button, 2" diameter. $100-125.

1950s Elsie flicker pin-back button, 1.5" diameter. $50-60.

Fold-over, tin tab buttons from the 1950s-1960s. $10-15 each.

1950s Elsie daisy pin with 1940s ribbon. Elsie pin, $25-30. Ribbon, $10-15.

1949 Elsie buttons on original cards, 4" x 3". $65-75 per set.

Late 1940s cool and hard to find Elsie and children hair clips, 2" long. $65-75 each.

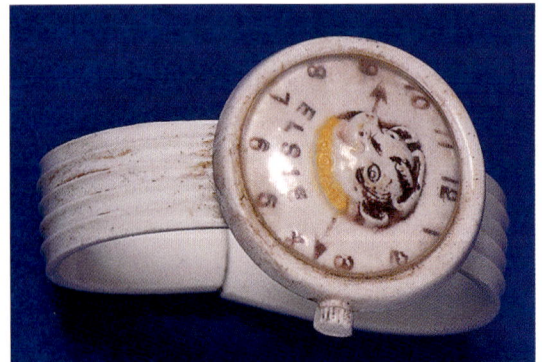

Late 1940s plastic Elsie toy wrist watch. The face is 1" in diameter. $50-60.

Late 1940s plastic Elsie toy pin-back watch on original card, 1" in diameter. $75-100. Watch only, $30-35.

1950s plastic Elsie toy rings. $25-30 each.

1950s Elsie tie clasp on original card, 'Borden's Billion Boosters,' 1.75" long. $35-40.

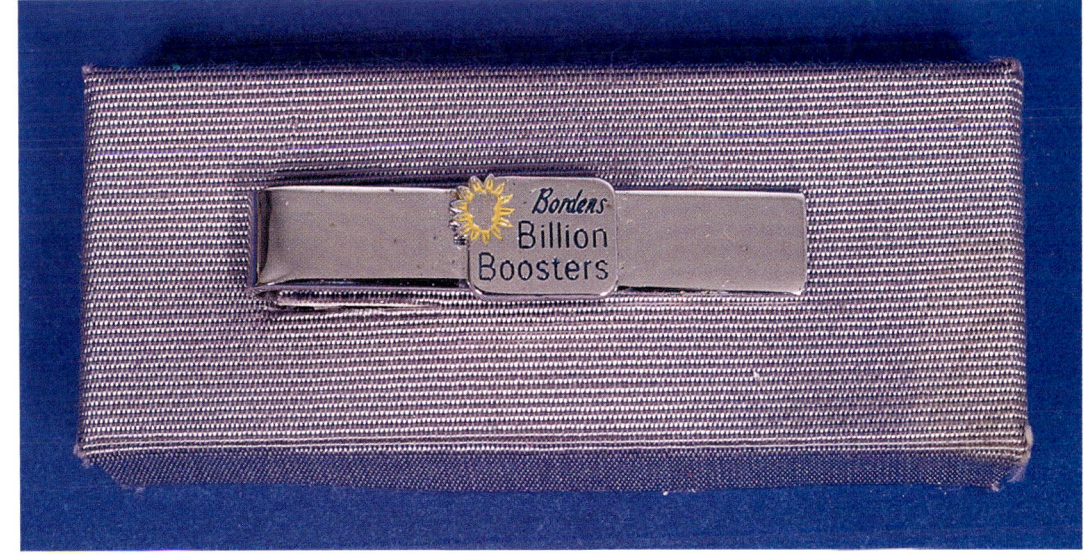

1950s Elsie tie clasp in the original box, 2.5" long. $65-75.

1950s Elsie key chain in the original box, 1" in diameter. $65-75.

1950s Elsie tie clasps and key chains. $25-30 each.

Pocket knife, 2.25" long, from the 1950s, $40-45. 1950s Elsie money clip with knifes, 2" long. $45-50.

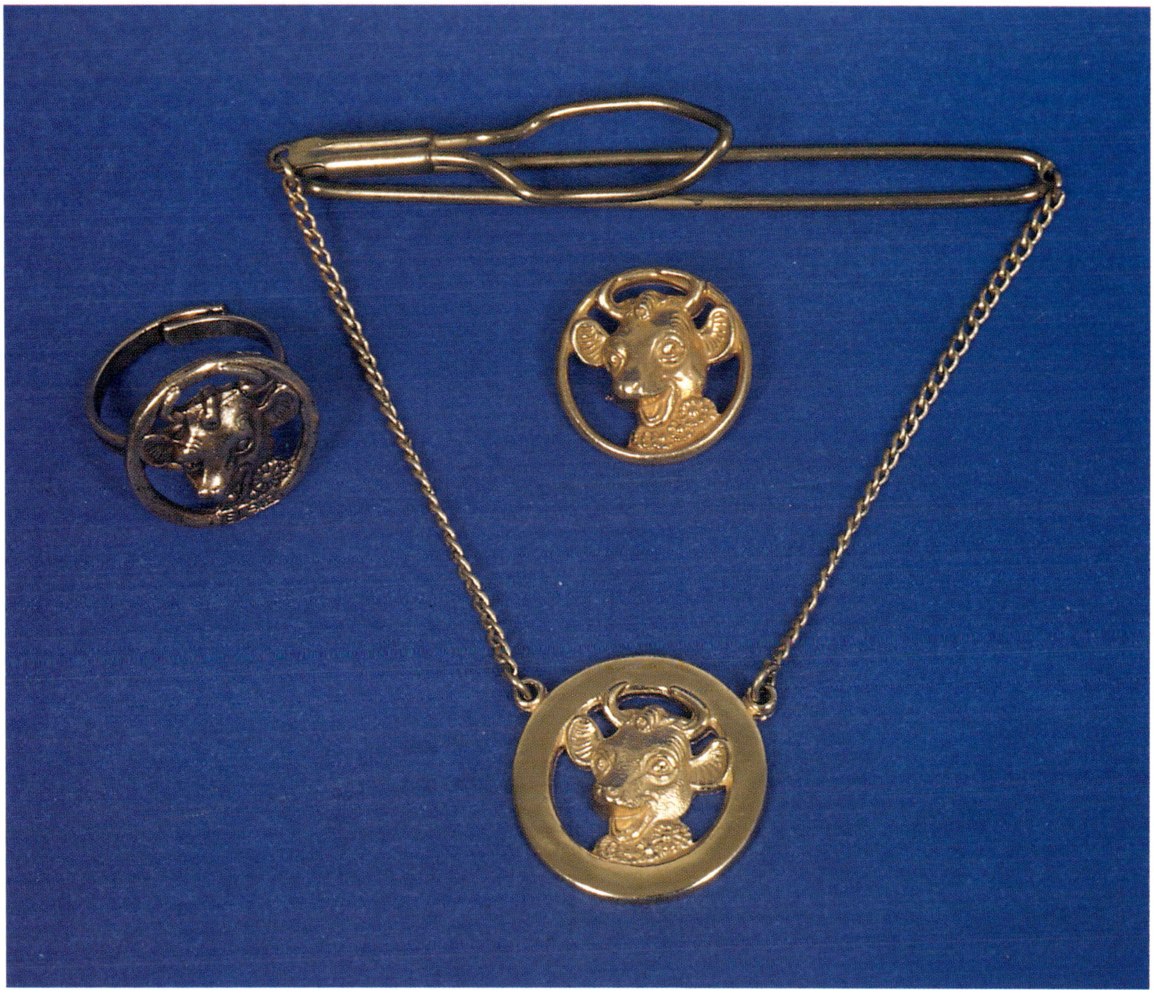

1950s Elsie metal ring, pin, and hanging tie clasp. Ring, $25-30. Pin, $15-20. Tie clasp, $45-50.

1957 Elsie compact, 2.5" x 3". $75-95.

1950s Elsie earrings in their original box, 0.75" in diameter. $65-75. Earrings only, $25-30.

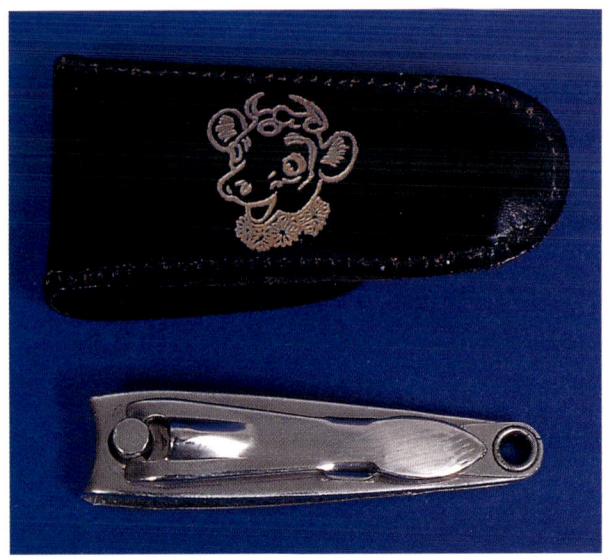

1950s Elsie nail clippers, 2.5" long. $25-30.

1950s Borden's 'Good Food Line' plastic train whistle, 3" long. $25-30.

1950s Borden's match books. $25-30.

1950s Elsie Hyde Park pottery ash tray, 10" x 5". $175-200.

1950s Elsie Hyde Park pottery ash tray, 8.5" x 5.5". $175-200.

From left to right: Sapphire, Imperial, and Narudan brand cigarette lighters with Elsie's picture, from the 1950s. They are 2" long and value $40-45 each.

Hard-to-find 1940s Elmer cigarette lighter made by Park, 2" tall. $75-95.

1950s Zippo brand Elsie cigarette lighter, 2" tall. In fair condition, $65-75.

1950s Elsie Zippo brand cigarette lighter, 2" tall. Mint in original box, $300-350. Lighter only, $125-150.

1950s Elsie Zippo brand cigarette lighter, 2" tall. Mint in original box, $300-350. Lighter only, $125-150.

1950s Lufkin brand 6' measuring tape, 1.5". In original box, $125-150. Tape only, $65-75.

Six 1950s Elsie pen and mechanical pencils, $45-50 each. Pen, mint in the box, $65-75.

1950s Elsie floating mechanical pencils. Elsie pencil on the left is 5" long, and the object is to try to get Elsie's daisy wreath over her head. Elsie pencil on the right is a floating scoop of ice cream and you must try to get the scoop of ice cream level in the cone. Both valued at $65-75 each.

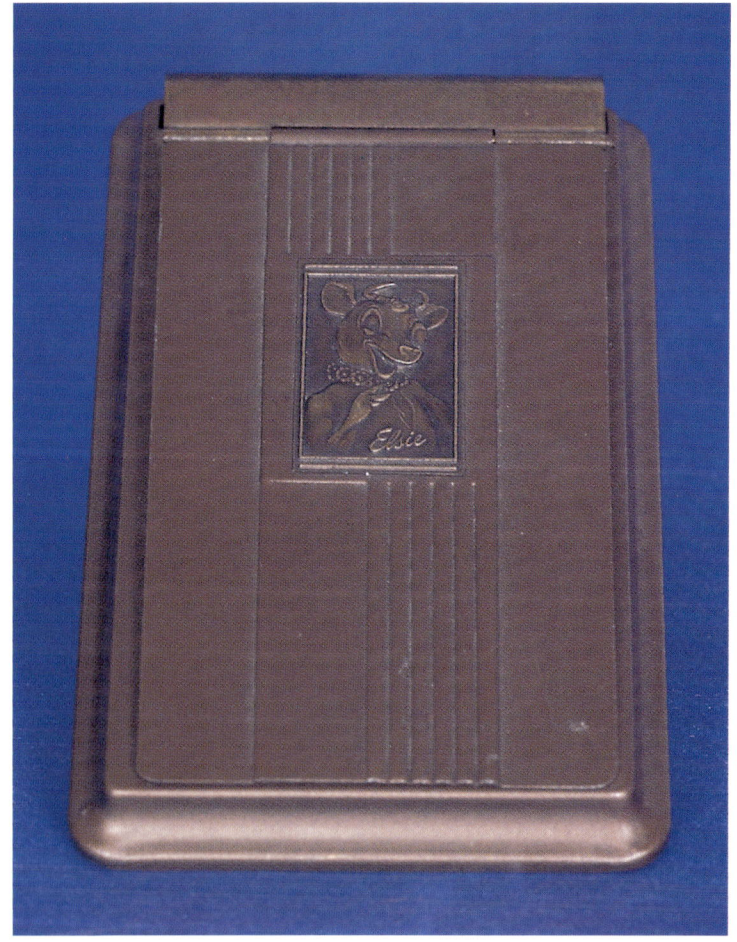

Early 1940s, metal Elsie clip-board, 6" x 3.5". $65-75.

146

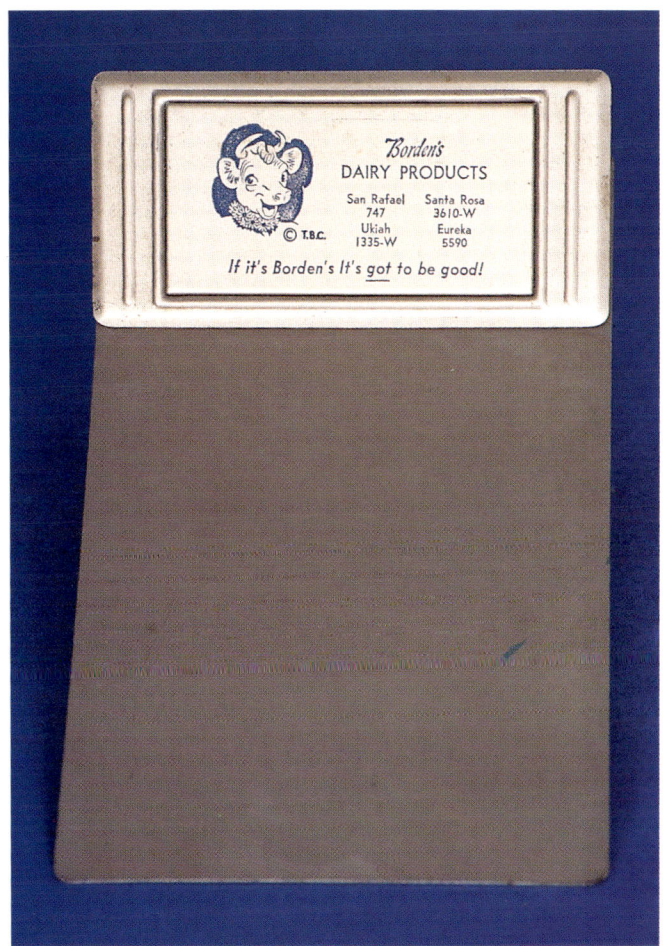

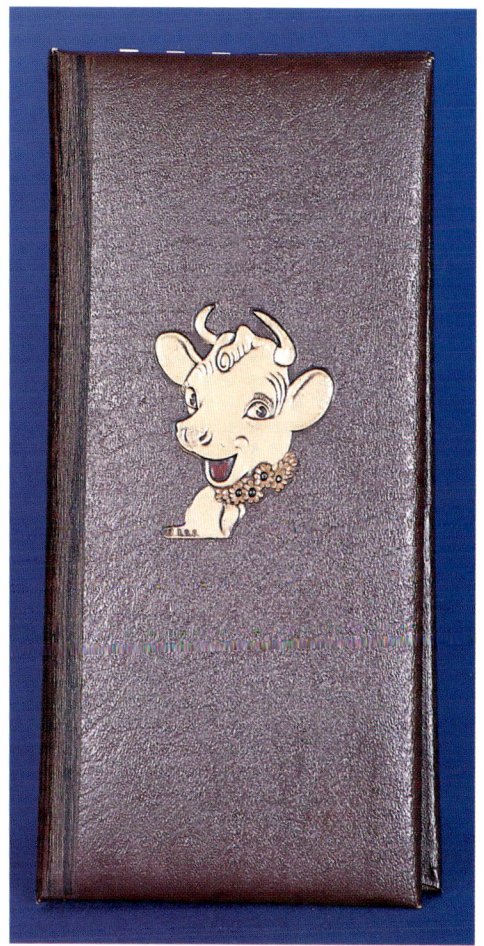

Late 1940s, metal Elsie clip-board, 9" x 5.5". $65-75.

Late 1940s, mint, Elsie leather telephone index pad, 10" x 5". $125-150.

Early 1960s, Hilton brand bowling shirt with Elsie patch on the back. $100-125.

Chapter Four

Original Art Work & Unique Items

This area of collecting is the most exciting, yet it encompasses items that are the hardest to find. Over the years of searching and tracking down countless leads we have obtained some of our most treasured and favorite items and met many nice people on our travels. David Reid is one of those people. David started working with Borden's in 1939, the same year Elsie made her first public appearance at the New York World's Fair. David later flew a WWII U.S. bomber, while stationed in Europe, called *The Milk Run* with Elsie's picture painted on the side. After the war he became Borden's advertising manager for fluid milk and ice cream. As an artist he designed many magazine ads promoting Borden's products and helped design the famous 1951 Daisy logo. He created the 100th Year Centennial Design for Borden's in 1957. We would like to thank David for the time he spent identifying the artists of our original art work and all his wonderful stories.

Early 1950s original magazine art by Walter Early. This 29" x 22" drawing is of 'Elsie's Good Food Line Train.' Walter Early did many drawings for the Borden Company. This original drawing is valued at $1,000-1,500.

Here is a record sleeve with a print of the original drawing done by Walter Early. This sleeve is 9.5" x 9.5" and contains 'Elsie's Good Food Line,' promotional, 78 RPM record from 1952. $65-75.

Mid 1950s original magazine art by Tore Aspland. Size of this drawing is 17" x 17.5" with matting. This drawing is of Beulah, and is pictured on a 1958 calendar that I have. $650-700.

1958 calendar with the print of the original drawing by Tore Aspland. Beulah is on the far right. $40-50.

Late 1940s to 1950s original magazine art by Tore Aspland. Size of this drawing is 23" x 21.5". $500-600.

Late 1940s to 1950s original magazine art by Cliff Hartley. The size is 21" x 14.5". $600-700.

Late 1950s original magazine art by Frank Jonson. The size of this drawing is 21" x 16" and is pictured on a 1960 calendar that I have. One of our favorites! $850-1,000.

1960 calendar with print of the original art by Frank Jonson. $50-60.

Late 1940s to 1950s original magazine art by David Reid. Size of this drawing is 22" x 15". $500-600.

Hand-painted, original ink drawing by Cliff Hartley. Looks to be from the late 1950s to early 1960s, 20" x 16" with matting. $350-400.

Hand-painted, original ink drawing by Cliff Hartley. Looks to be from the late 1950s to early 1960s, 20" x 16" with matting. $350-400.

Mid 1960s original magazine art, 18.5" x 17.5".
Artist Unknown. $300-350.

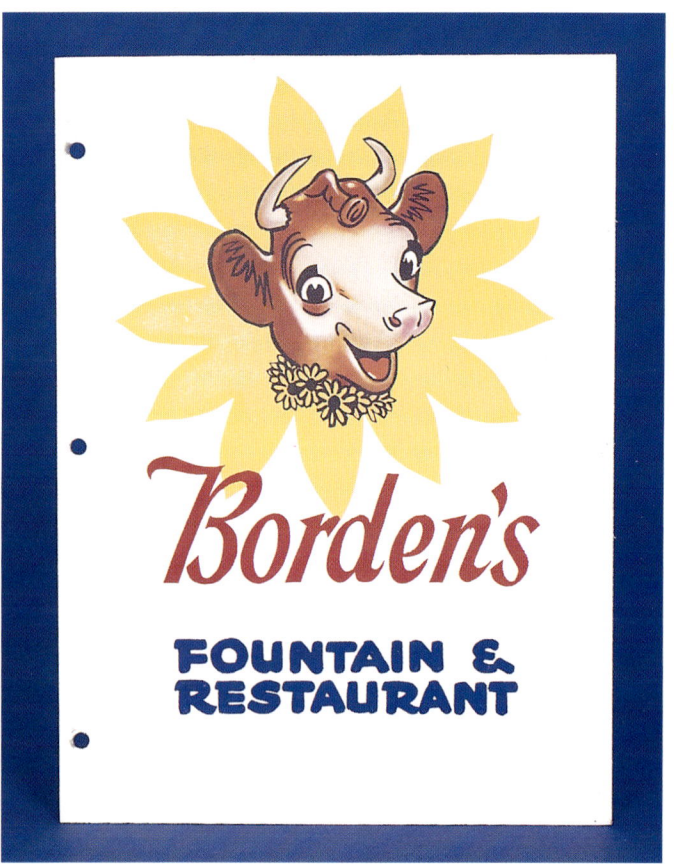

Late 1950s hand-painted art work for soda fountain display, 11" x 8". $100-150.

Large, 68" x 47", framed, cardboard store display from the late 1940s to early 1950s. $450-500.

Large, 10' x 3', paper, corrugated store display with wooden frame on the back. These signs were built right in the store with prefabricated materials. Very few have survived over the years. I got a good deal on this sign from a friend of mine years ago, and he reminds me of this every time I see him. Thanks Bo! $750-800.

Late 1940s Elsie mechanical store display. When you plug her in, her mouth begins to chew her cud and she makes the appropriate noises. She stands 33" tall and is 24" wide. Her head and body are made of soft rubber. $2,000-2,500.

1950s rotating Borden's cottage cheese display. When turned on, the wooden base rotates around to advertise the product. Wooden base is 32" in diameter. Cardboard display on top is 17" in diameter and 11.5" tall. $650-700.

154

Above: Rare 1950s Elsie battery animated store display. When turned on, Elsie winks her eye and moves her mouth. She stands 35" tall and 26" wide. $650-700.

Right: Late 1950s Elsie chair looks to be a display of some kind. I have seen the pillow before but never a chair. Could be made for a special event or promotion? Pillow alone is valued at $150-200. Pillow with chair, $400-450.

1957 Borden's salesman promotion books picturing all the cool promotional products available to the Borden's clientele and potential clients. $350-400 each.

Large 1950s Borden's store display using a carnival mirror, to help promote their healthy products. Hand-painted, wooden panels, with a large neon sign on top. 8' tall x 7' wide. This is a one of a kind, $4,000-4,500.

Rare, wooden, Borden's ice cream cart. This cart was made to sell ice cream along the sidewalk. From the 1950s, 38" tall x 26" wide x 22" deep. Hand crafted and painted, $1,500-1,800.

Several select pictures of pages from the 1957 salesman promotion books. Gives you an idea of the creative advertising available to soda fountains and local grocery stores. Also available for ordering through your district salesman were several types of Borden's premiums.

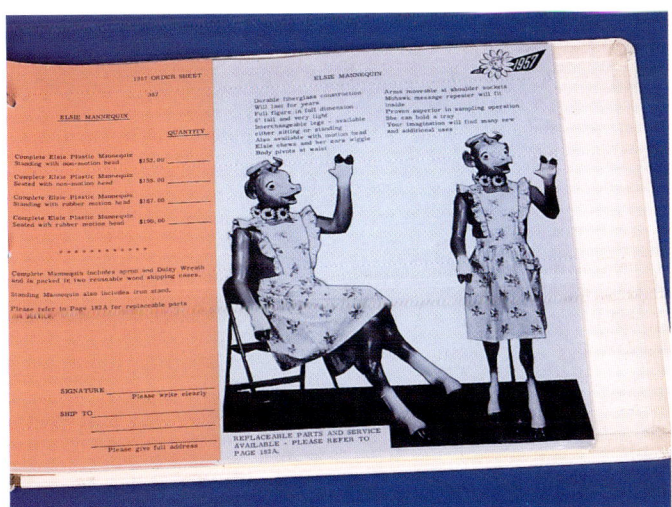
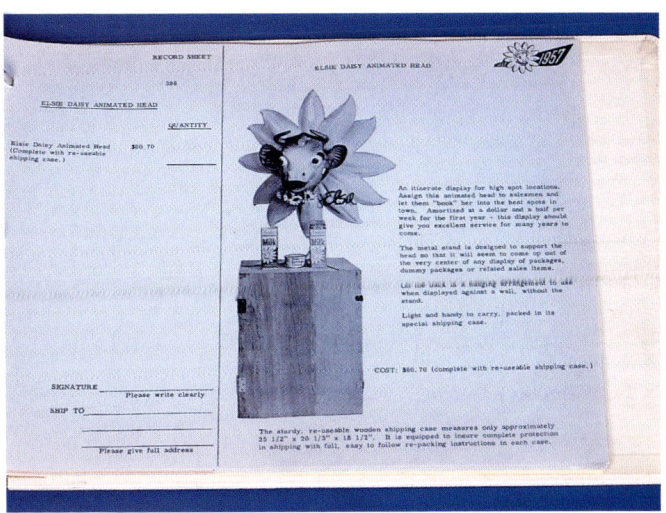

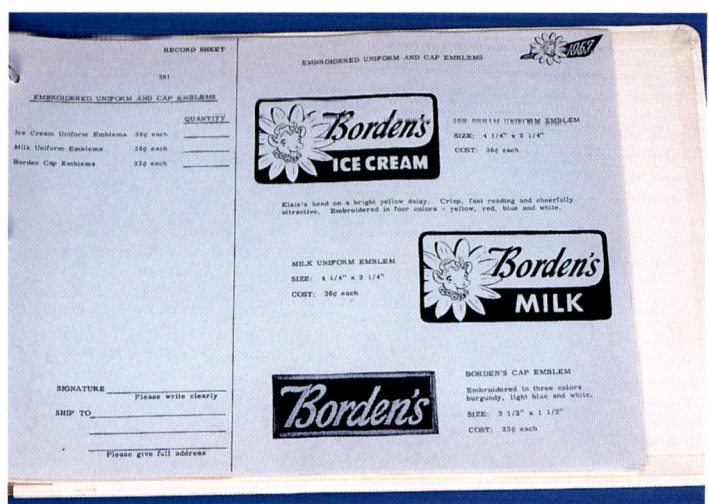

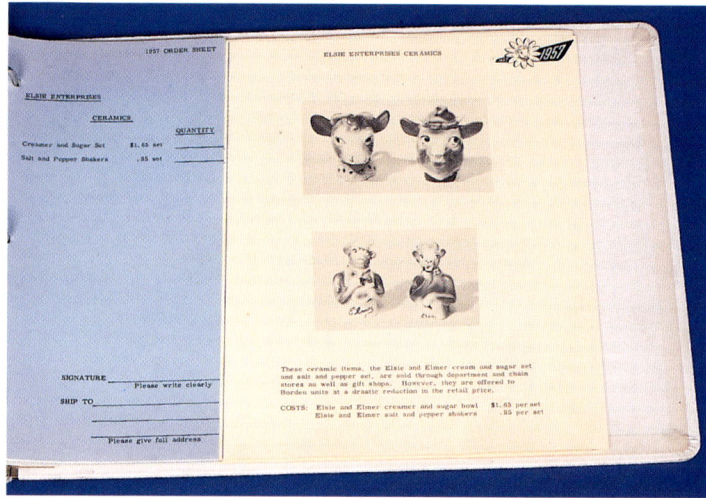

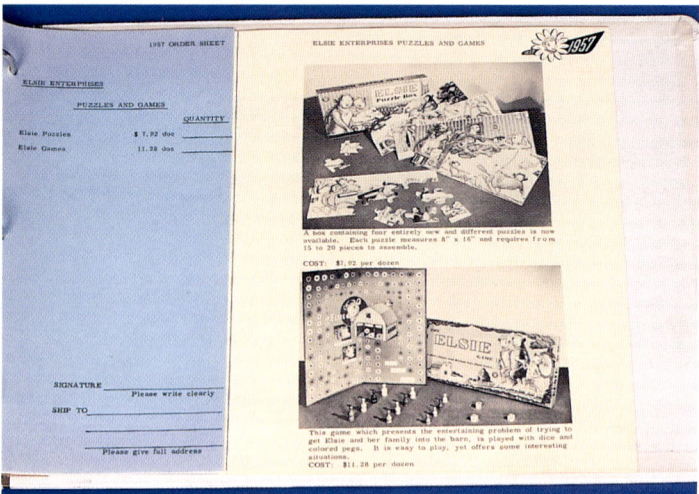

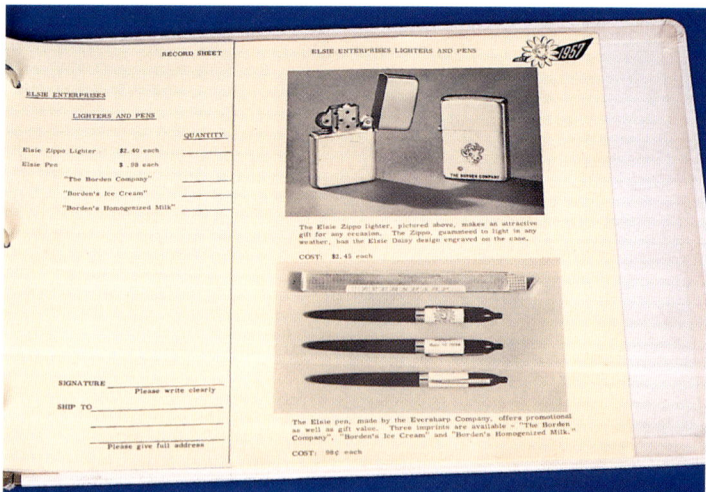

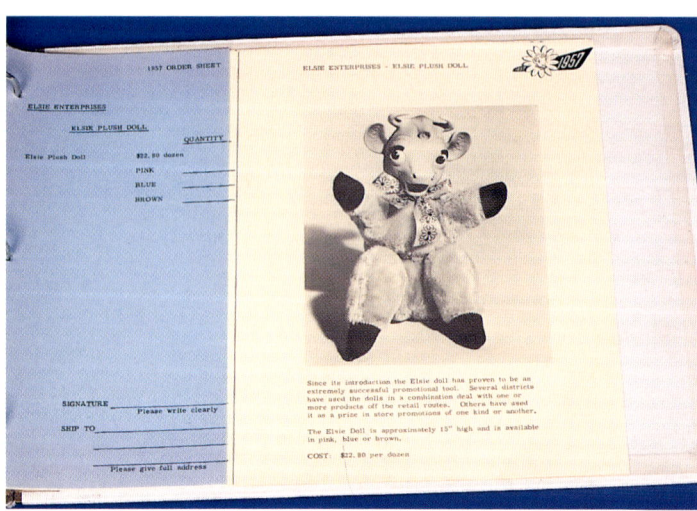

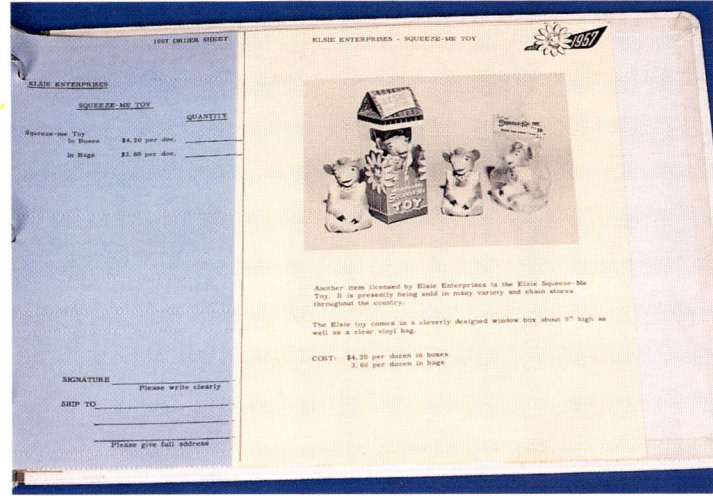

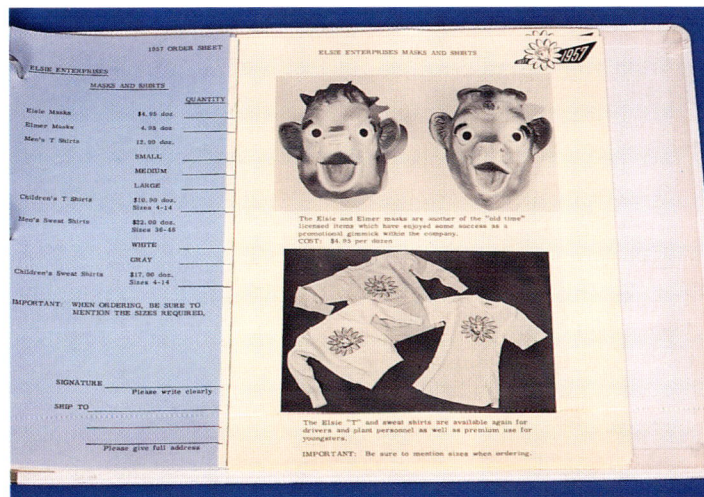

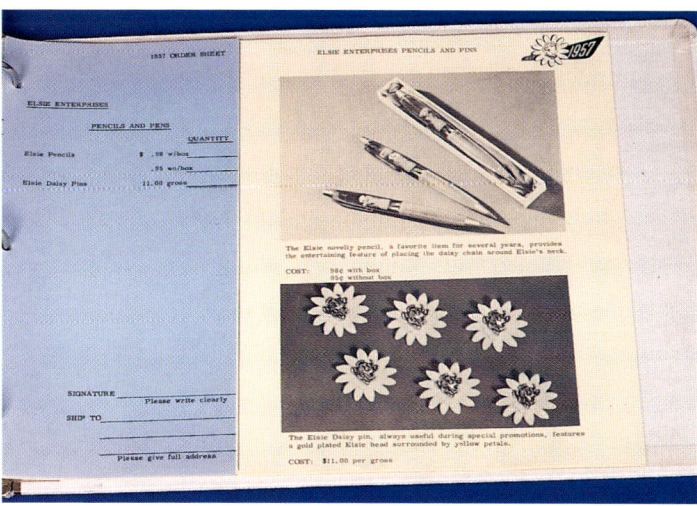

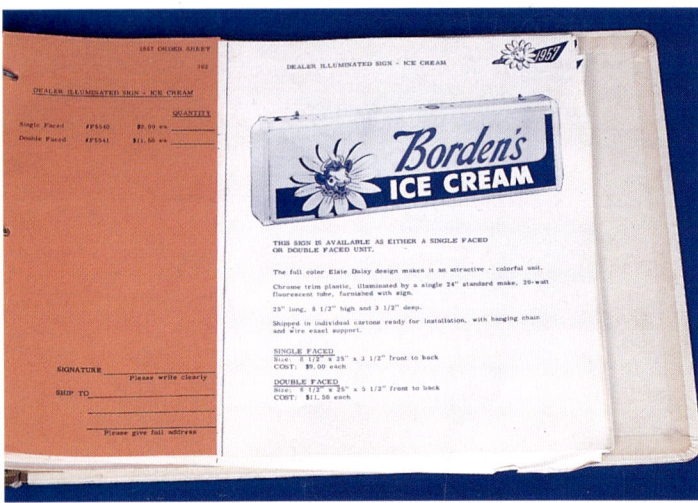

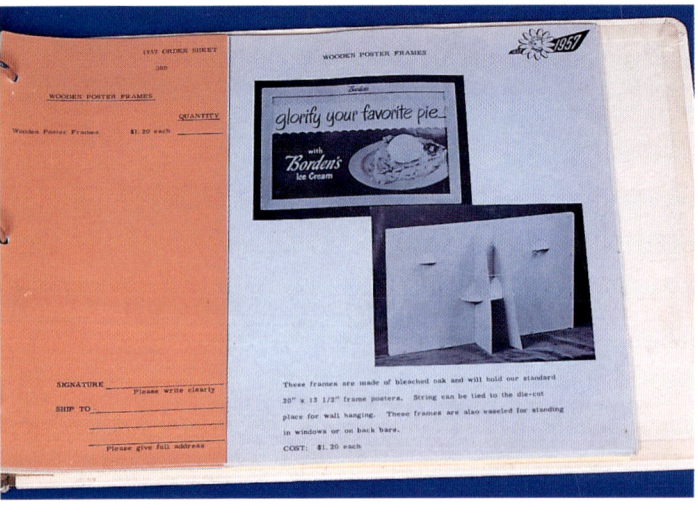